THE STORY OF ME A BLACK NURSE

By Diane Jones RN

authorHOUSE®

AuthorHouse™
1663 Liberty Drive
Bloomington, IN 47403
www.authorhouse.com
Phone: 1-800-839-8640

ISBN: 978-1-4567-2717-8 (sc)
ISBN: 978-1-4567-2718-5 (e)

About The Author

Restore the "Art of Caring" and promote a spirit of "Excellence" to the Nursing Profession. I hope and pray some how to provoke and motivate some of you to re-light this torch and carry it to the finish line.

Diane Jones has served the public for thirty years, first as a Certified Nursing Assistant, next as a Licensed Vocational Nurse, and now as Registered Nurse. Over the years, she has been both amazed with the benefits of advanced medical technology and troubled by the decline in the ability of health care professionals to actually "Care" for the people they care for.

When she entered the Healthcare Profession she vowed to herself that she would never compromise her values as a nurse and she would give her patients the best care possible regardless of race or creed. She would "Care" for people.

In- spite of many obstacles, she has kept that vow.

The accounts I give are written according to the best of my memory and are not intended to implicate any person or agency. They are given to memorialize my experiences and hopefully prepare or encourage someone else to face the harsh realities of my profession. The names of persons and businesses have been changed or omitted to protect my interest, my family and my publisher from any retaliation by any who may feel the need to do so. My employee records have been included to lend credibility to the accounts I have shared.

Sincerely,

Diane S. Jones RN

Diane Jones RN

Forward

The Master Maker in his making, created Diane Shanell Jones, one of Gods true warriors.

Diane and I met three years ago. We worked as sister Director of Nurses in skilled care facilities that were jointly owned. We are and always will be friends. I think of myself as her second mother and she is my second daughter, my rock of Judah, my calm in the time of storms. She helps me pray and remain strong in times of stress, especially from a nursing viewpoint.

This is a sequel in her on-going saga. The life she writes about does not seem real at times but real it was and real it remains. There were some sorrowful memories. On the positive side, there were many more times of laughter and pure joy for her successes over the evils she faced.

When Diane gave me the honor of writing the Forward for this book "The Story of Me-A Black Nurse, I was truly humbled, surprised and very proud. "The Story of Me" was the beginning. In it she tells a sometimes awkward love story about a truly remarkable woman of God who in-spite of pain and sorrow has triumphed.

The struggles and barriers she met and overcame give hope to all females of color. She tells you, if you believe and trust in God you can and will find success and happiness regardless of life's obstacles. You will realize that like the tiny mustard seed, you can grow and become a stately gracious tree.

What I loved instantly about this book was the strength and determination of this lady. She was and still remains truly invested in her ability to help others live to become the best they can be. She believes in the pledge all nurses make to always give their best, be truthful and never do harm to any of Gods creatures, regardless of how you may personally feel inside. Sometimes she takes you into deep dark places and all you can think about is escape. Then she leads you out of that place with laughter and you rejoice in her victory. You often see yourself and people you have known or worked with and you understand her joys and her fears while you celebrate her successes. You cheer as she moves forward in her quest for a good life for others', herself and for her family.

You realize that the nursing profession is not like "General Hospital" of television fame but often a hurtful profession where your friends will turn on you in a heart beat for their own personal advancement. Then she shows you how belief in the truth and faith in a just God can and will help you overcome all adversaries.

Minister Jones's life story affirms and celebrates the life of a Black Professional in a time when the so called glass ceiling is really a concrete wall, a wall that all people of color in the nursing profession are busy creating cracks and openings in today.

You go girl!

Keep your story strong and maybe I'll be asked to write the afterword of your third book when it develops about the life of this remarkable lady called "Me."

Love you dearly

Mary L. Numa RN

Chapter 1

Are you a dreamer? I am. I am not asking if you have hopes and dreams. I am referring to dreams you have in the night, dreams when you sleep. For a long time I didn't have dreams. If I did, I didn't remember having them. I started dreaming again at a time in my life when I was under a great strain and was feeling very despondent.

I was working as a Licensed Vocational Nurse at a big hospital in Santa Barbara California. I was working twelve- hour shifts, full time hours and going to school full time to become a Registered Nurse.

I was newly divorced with a pre-teen aged daughter. Wanting to be closer to the school I would be attending, I relocated to the Santa Barbara area. I'd lost my home due to divorce. I started school and a new job almost simultaneously. The bills were piling up. Creditors were calling. I started having dreams about a flood coming to my city. Waters rising around my home forced me to climb higher and higher until I was at the top of my home outside on the roof. The flooding was relentless! Soon the waters overtook me and I was going under! Then I would wake up.

The dream was profound because that was exactly how I was feeling. Gasping and fighting the wicked waves I struggled to keep my head above water. Although I was able to swim I was very afraid of being under water.

That time in my life was very dark, full of change and unfamiliar territory. In spite of the many obstacles I faced I completed the RN Program at Santa Barbara City College. This is the story of how I made this journey, the struggles and rewards that followed told from my perspective as a Black nurse in a White owned and operated industry.

I really don't even know why I chose the medical profession. I seemed to fall into it. Was it my destiny? I believe it was because I believe we all have a destiny. I believe we gravitate towards things such as careers that we were meant to do because somewhere inside of us we were meant to do what we are doing. I have experienced a love maybe love is to strong a word "like" hate relationship with my career choice almost from day one.

Like many Blacks in America I came from an under privileged background. In my case I was not always under privileged. I was born into a military family. My father was a Technical Sergeant in the United States Air Force my mother a Home Maker. We traveled and lived in different countries, states, and towns. This provided me with a broader view of life and people in general. We had a normal in some ways more than normal upbringing until alcohol abuse and mental illness destroyed our home. We became wards of the court. I ended up in a foster home with my four brothers and sister.

Up to that point, there were no professional people in my life. There were no college graduates at least not in my immediate family circle. I don't even recall having the examples of hard working lay people in my environment. My grandparents were hard working but I only lived with them for short periods thus they didn't have that great an influence on my work ethics or career choices. Some of the other people in my life included but were not limited to pimps, drug addicts, high school dropouts, high school graduates and welfare dependents.

There were positive influences in my life on a small scale. My foster mother "Granny" was a churchgoer. She was the mother of our church. She took us in even though she was disabled from a Stroke. She found a home for us and gave us a somewhat normal life.

I was in high school when I decided to enter the medical profession. The school offered a Certified Nursing Assistant Program. I would soon be graduating from high school and I needed some sort of job skills to be able to provide for myself. It was what you might call a practical decision. I took the course and acquired my CNA Certificate. That was in 1980. My first job was at a convalescent home. I was very quiet and shy. I did my work and went home. I don't have vivid memories of that experience.

A Certified Nursing Assistant is the first level care provider in the nursing chain of command. At that time it consisted of a minimum six-week course that taught basic bedside care skills and principles. These skills included task such as showering, bathing, feeding, changing diapers and charting requirements. My course was a bit more extensive. I can't be exact but I believe it was a school semester. We were taught theory which included the basic Anatomy and Physiology of each body system, the effects of aging and basic skills for caring for the acutely ill and the elderly person. We trained in nursing homes and at acute care hospitals.

Prior to this time it was not necessary to be certified to work in a nursing home or hospital. This position was known as a Nursing Assistant, also known as (AKA) NA. You learned the job on the job. As a standard you were given two days of orientation to the facility then you were on your own. This was the standard for CNA's too. My patient load was usually ten, twelve or more on the day shift. The times I worked evenings I would have twenty- five or so patients. At times I worked the graveyard shift and had fifty patients to take care of because we were short staffed. On these nights I began my rounds usually by eleven thirty PM. By the time I finished the first round it was time to start the next one around two AM. Making rounds consisted of checking on my patients, taking their vital signs, changing their diapers if needed and turning them. Back then we called diapers diapers. Now we call them briefs. On the morning shift I remember having to wash and dress most of my patients, get them up, take them to the dining room, some by wheelchair, others walked with help to breakfast, feed several of them, lay them down for naps, take the remaining ones to activities, give showers and change them, take them back to the dining room for lunch, feed again, lay them down for naps, do your charting and go home. We did not have the fancy equipment and supplies that are available today. We used our own muscles for transferring and lifting. There were no hydraulic lifts, gait belts or special mattresses. We used cloth diapers that we had to rinse out not disposable briefs. We did not use gloves. We washed our own linen and diapers for re-use. Yes in those days we used safety pins to pin their diapers just like you would use on a baby when diapering them. In addition to our routine duties we had special assignments such as cleaning the shower rooms, laundry duty or cleaning the break-room. Bedpans and basins were made of metal. They were sterilized and packaged for re-use too. We were supposed to accomplish this in an eight- hour day. For the most part we did.

Some of my patients were senile, some oriented. They ranged from ambulatory to bed ridden and from nice to mean and cantankerous. In those days it was common to see patients with huge smelly bedsores and nasal gastric feeding tubes (NGT). We were required to aid our patient's bowel function when they were not able to do it themselves. That meant putting on a pair of gloves, applying lubrication to ones finger, placing the finger in the rectum and digging the feces out. It was hard work. Most of our patients did not have family involvement. It broke my heart to see them in the condition they were in with no one to visit and love them. I remember thinking way back then that one day I would like to own a facility of my own so I could run it right.

At some point during that time period I got married. I was eighteen. Over the next five years I worked as a CNA in various convalescent homes. By this time I'd been spit at, yelled at, cursed, hit and pinched. I began to feel like a butt wiper instead of an aide. A few of the patients were appreciative. Most of them acted as though they expected and deserved care. I still have a vivid memory of a very heavy, very slow moving, white female patient. Her voice was deep and monotone, whose name I can't mention. She would demand things of the staff not ask. "Put me on the toilet." "Wipe my butt." When I tried to encourage her to wipe her own butt (she had full use of both arms and hands) she clearly let me know that was my job! Of course I had to do it if she refused to which she always did. One particular day she even told me "go back to Africa where you belong." She was upset with me for trying to encourage her to help herself. I had not dealt with much racial bias up to that point in my life so I was actually surprised and truly offended by her remarks. I replied "I've been told that there were bigots in this country but up till now I had not met one". "So it is true"? They do exist! Naturally she did not like my response. I did not care. I really wanted to slap her, old or not she was a racist. I did not slap her but I did tell my supervisor of my feelings. I did not have to take care of her the rest of that day.

During that time period I worked at several different facilities trying to find better pay and better working conditions. The wage was only around 4.75/hour, not very much for this type of work. Once I was even fired from a job because a White lady in the business office falsely accused me of slapping a patient. This is what really happened. The business office was across the hall from a small activity/dining room. I went into the activity room to retrieve one of my patients so I could take her to be cleaned up after lunch. She always got food all over her clothing. She began yelling and cursing at me. She was known for this behavior as well as for pinching. She was confused. I was taught special techniques to keep from being pinched like how to distract her on one side while doing something else on the other side i.e. give her something to hold, when she reached for the new item take the cup away. She was holding a cup of coffee at the time. I explained to her that it was time to go back to her room so she could be cleaned up. She politely threw her cup of coffee at me and screeched and yelled as though I was killing her. I was startled. Again, I wanted to slap her but refrained from doing so. Instead I took the cup from her (thank God the contents were no longer hot) I then removed her bib and took her back to her room to change her. If my memory serves me well the visibility from the business office to the inside of the room where we were was not clear. The next day when I arrived to work I was called into the Director of Nursing (DON) office. She told me someone in the business office accused me of slapping a patient. With my check already prepared she told me I was fired. I denied the allegations. I told her the only thing that happened on the day she was referring to was that a patient threw coffee on me and I grabbed the cup in an attempt to prevent her from throwing the coffee on me! It may have appeared to some one that I struck someone but I did not! I told her to check the patient for red marks or evidence of a slap. She refused to check. My explanation was dismissed. Just like that I was dismissed. The experience was upsetting for me but at that time I was a very introverted type person. I took it in stride and moved on. About a year later the DON called me to apologize for the mix up. She told me that they later learned that my accuser had an alcohol abuse problem and had apparently made up other things that were later found to be untrue. She offered my job back to me. I took it. I did not stay long though. Now the staffing was horrible. I was working the night shift and taking care of twenty-five to fifty patients. I was already experiencing burn out and had seriously considered leaving the medical field. Instead of leaving the field some of my relatives encouraged me to go back to school to become a Licensed Vocational Nurse (LVN). This begins a new chapter in my life and my nursing career.

Chapter 2

My marriage was not good. I did not have a loving supportive husband to take care of my daughter and me. I'd been separated from my husband for a year. He decided after only a year that he did not love me any more. He asked me to leave our apartment. I was dumbfounded and desperate to make things work but finally complied with his wishes. I hoped we would get back together but realized he was serious when I found his new girlfriend in the apartment that we once shared together. Defeated I moved back to my hometown. I hung out with a few guys, some friends and took up modeling lessons. The modeling lessons served to build my self–esteem. It was fun but soon I realized I wasn't really going anywhere. I was separated but not divorced. I had loose ends, unfinished business that I needed to take care of in my life. It was time for me to make our separation official so I could move on or give my marriage another try. I would live to regret my decision but I decided to give it another try.

Shortly after reconciling with my husband I became pregnant. My daughter was two months old when I started the nursing program. I went on welfare at my husband's insistence. He made it clear that he was not going to support me. It was the systems duty to do that not his. We were together but not together if you know what I mean.

I thought about being an LVN right out of high school. There was a vocational college in my area that offered LVN training. I tested for the program and did not pass the entrance exam. Now married, a new mother and burned out with being a CNA, I was ready to try again. I scheduled another appointment to retake the test. During my follow-up interview I learned that I passed the entrance exam. I was happy but explained that I'd tried one time before to pass the entrance exam and failed. The man conducting the interview voiced his surprise. He stated that the test had been changed to a different style but with the test scores I got this time he didn't understand how I failed the first time. The current test was more difficult. I often wondered if there was foul play involved the first time I'd taken the test. But I did not spend too much time worrying about it. I was in! This time I did it!

Starting the LVN program was not totally exciting for me. It was the next logical step to take to improve my financial situation. I had to eat and pay my bills. I had a baby to think about.

The school offered two types of programs. The most attractive option to me was the full- time program. It was a Monday through Friday program. Taking the full-time program meant I could finish in one year. The other option was a part-time program, this included one theory day and two clinical days a week. It would take two years to complete. It was less attractive but more practical. I chose the part time program. I applied for and received financial aide that paid for the whole program. It cost somewhere around $7000.00. Coming from an underprivileged background this was truly a blessing for me. The other good thing about it was I was not required to make any reimbursement payments until a year after I finished the program.

My support system consisted of my Granny (foster mom) and one of my younger brothers. They kept my daughter for me when I went to school. I paid my brother for babysitting. They were so cute together. My brother was around nine or ten years old so Granny was the real responsible one, the brains behind the operation. We just thought it would be a good way for my brother to make some pocket change and being disabled Granny needed a little bit of help. My little brother helped to carry, change and feed my baby girl. He was the muscle behind the operation. Yes they were a good, no great pair! I would not have made it through the program if it were not for the both of them.

I can't remember how many students were actually in my class. I don't feel the need to be that exact. I think we had about fifteen students. Of those fifteen there were only three black students myself included. Over the years I would find this ratio to be the norm. This norm would become very disturbing to me. Of the fifteen we had one male student. He was Black. His name was Perry. Then there was Belinda and myself.

Perry was younger then Belinda and myself. He was single and still lived at home. He was dark complexioned, charming and playful. I guess you could say he had attitude and style. He didn't take things to seriously you know. He didn't sweat the small stuff. He drove his own car. Unlike Belinda or me, he grew up in a well-off family. They had a big nice home. He lived with both his parents and his siblings. He invited me to his home for a family function. I remember they had a pool table and nice furnishings. I was impressed.

Belinda like me married young. She had a son and was trying to make it in life. She was nice and attractive with a fair medium complexion. We both had spiritual backgrounds. I came from a Pentecostal background, she from a Seventh Day Adventist background. Sometimes we got on Perry's case about taking things so lightly and playing around too much. One of the pleasant memories I have of Belinda was that she made the best-looking salads. When we went to lunch at the hospital during our clinical rotations she always made salads with eggs, croutons, three- bean medley, cheese and other toppings. This was new to me. I was not into salads at that time. My Granny fixed cooked vegetables like green beans, cabbage, greens, corn and carrots. My mother made salads but they were plain with Iceberg Lettuce and Tomatoes. Yes I still remember the way she made a salad. I make mine the way she made them to this day.

I liked both of them. They became my partners at school. For some reason we rarely socialized outside of school though. Even though my marriage was on again off again and my husband was often gone he was the jealous type. I didn't know Belinda's husband but I felt he was the jealous type or should I say the possessive type too.

Our class was diverse. We had White students, Hispanic students, young and older students. Our teacher was a retired Nunn. She was the Theory instructor. I think she told us she was Jewish and she had a military back- ground. She was short with a Boston type accent. She wore her hair cut short and neat. But there was nothing small about her personality. She told us old stories about her nurse training days. Sometimes she told us that we drove her to drink! On the nights she had to grade test she sometimes needed a little help from "Jack Daniels" if you know what I mean. She made us laugh. She chewed us out when necessary. She felt like a friend but clearly she was our teacher.

You got your CNA certificate if you past the first six weeks of the program. I already had that so I breezed through that part of the course. Everyone passed that part of the course. That was one of the special things about being in the class. We shared each other's triumphs and defeats. When test results came out we huddled around asking, "What did you get?" "What did you get?"

Highlights of the program that I can recall include the first time that I cared for a little old Black man. I don't remember his medical diagnosis. We were supposed to research the diagnosis, history and medications of each of our patients. We were supposed to research any test that they'd had or were going to have. The teacher might ask us questions about our patients at any time during the clinical day so we had to be prepared. Clinical was the term for the time we actually spent in the hospital setting. I don't remember any of that information about this little Black man. I do remember that he'd been there for several days now. I had to give him a bed bath. He was so dirty and his skin was so dry. His toe nails were long and dirty too. I had to change the water several times before I was done. I remember how sad and angry I felt about his condition. If he'd been there for several days already why was he so dirty? Didn't the other nurses who were assigned to him before me clean him up? It was obvious to me that they hadn't. I felt surely that his neglect was due to the fact that he was Black. He was probably unkempt when he was admitted. I did not see any excuse for his continued lack of care after all he was in a hospital. He was very quiet and mild mannered. The experience stood out in my mind so much that this later became a pet peeve of mine. When providing care or teaching students to provide care, I made sure that feet and toes were thoroughly cleaned and lotion offered or applied to the patient.

There was the time I took care of a young man. I was not sure of his nationality. He wasn't Black. I don't think he was White either. He was a very new newly wed and was in an accident involving one of those ATC three wheelers. They were popular at that time. He was very good looking. He was lean and muscular. His wife was also very pretty. Both were brunettes. He suffered a neck fracture and was confined to one of those circular electric beds for months. This contraption allowed him to move his extremities but immobilized his neck. He had rods inserted into each side of his head connected to a circular piece called a Halo. The nurses had to clean the insertion sites daily with Beta dine to prevent infection. The contraption had a bed built into it so he could lye on his back when he was supposed to. Then the bed could be flipped over so that he was suspended prone at other times. This prevented bedsores and loss of mobility due to immobility. They had a lot of family support. Some days he was in good spirits some days he was depressed. He'd been in that contraption for some time and was getting tired of it. I had mixed feelings about this experience. I felt sorry for him and his wife. She handled things so well. I could see the love they had for each other. I was attracted to him because he was so good looking but I was also embarrassed to take care of him because he was a young man. He was in his twenties I'm sure. I was not used to the idea of a young person being in the hospital. He was blessed because the location of the fracture did not leave him paralyzed. His recovery was long but complete.

The first time I saw some one with projectile vomiting; now that was an experience! It surprised me and almost made me sick. Projectile vomiting is when a person forcefully throws up. In this case the patient a young White man had fallen from a high location. He was in the radiology department getting X-rays to determine whether he had internal injuries or not. He was lying on the gurney. The X-ray Tech went into the protected area. I was positioned in the protected area too. This was done to protect us from exposure to radiation. The room was very large. There was some sort of balcony area above the equipment area. Very unexpectedly the patient vomited an orange colored stream of stomach contents. He growled as the stream shot almost precisely up and across the room. It nearly reached the balcony. It was gross. A term we used in those days. I learned something else about myself that day. I was squeamish about any type of fluids or substances that came out of the mouth. Saliva, sputum, vomit and food particles they all made me gag. I had to learn to deal with this weakness though because unlike many of today's professionals we were taught not to show our displeasure or emotions about things such as this. We did not want to make the patient feel embarrassed. It was considered unprofessional.

At some point during the program one of our instructors took some time off for personal reasons. We had a substitute. She was young, attractive and Black. Wow! This was impressive and very uncommon.

I remember having one Black teacher in junior high school. I remember her because I was very irritated by her. She was my choir teacher. I enjoyed choir but for some reason that teacher got on my last nerve. I had a Black teacher in high school that I admired a great deal. She was also young and attractive. She was married. She dressed nice and I felt, had it going on. Her personality was out going. She taught a class that helped to prepare students for life on their own. It was designed to inspire ones thinking about things such as paying bills, furnishing a place to live and making a living. She complimented my work and told me that I was going to make it in life. Mrs. Thompson was her name.

It was not common to see Black students or employees in the nursing profession at least not where I lived. My school was in San Bernardino California. My clinical experience was in San Bernardino and Riverside California. So it was nice to see a Black instructor. Unfortunately I was not impressed for long. It was apparent that the instructor was intelligent and possessed a command and knowledge of the material but the class did not receive her well. She was curt and to the point. At times she was even condescending in her responses to the students. Perry who was generally laid back did not care for her approach. Now I must say that Perry was used to charming the other instructors but this one could not, would not be charmed. Some of the students complained about her and we never saw her again.

I'd been through many hardships by that time in my life but was not bitter. To understand my past you will need to read my autobiography "THE STORY OF ME". I did not have a chip on my shoulder from being abused so I didn't understand people who did have a chip on their shoulder. I didn't know this teacher but felt she had a chip on her shoulder, something to prove. I now think I can understand how she may have felt. I now believe that the chip may have been there because she was a young Black professional. I now know that being a Black professional in a White world is not easy! We are expected to be better than every one else but yet be like everyone else. This did not gain us respect but rather caused us extra grief. You have no real peer group. You don't fit in so you don't make friends easily. At that early age in my life I did not see these things quite this clearly but believe me I do now.

The program was not hard for me. I maintained a B average. My problems during the program were personal not professional.

One day while at school I went out to my car to get something. I don't remember what it was I needed but I found something I was not looking for. It was a card from someone my husband went out on a date with. It was very clear from the card that they shared a very special and intimate evening together. I was visibly disturbed by what I'd found. Perry and Belinda asked me what was wrong. I showed them the card. Belinda felt sorry for me. Perry was angry for me. He tried to convince me I deserved better. I decided to go home early that day. I could not concentrate any way. I wanted to talk to my Granny about what I'd found to see what she thought about it. Granny told me to watch his behavior when he arrived. That will tell you if he has something to hide. Sure enough, when he came to the house I was waiting for him. I was watching from the front window. I can't remember how he got there but our car a yellow Camaro was parked out front. He immediately went to our car and began searching for something. I knew what that something was. I knew it was the card he was looking for. Busted! He was cold busted! When he could not find it he came inside. Of course I showed him what he was looking for. He of course said it was not his. It belonged to a friend, someone he allowed to borrow the car. A likely story! I was hurt because this was not the first time he cheated on me. I had to stay focused though. I could not let this stop me from handling my business so I pressed forward.

It seemed that the more I pressed forward the more my husband acted out. He made it difficult for me every chance he got. There were times he would not show up in time for me to use the car to go to school, or he would wait till the last minute causing me to be on pins and needles worried about missing class or being late.

My husband was very controlling. During most of this time we did not have a phone. He said we could not afford a phone. He fussed if I used the heater. He said we could not afford to use the heater either. At the time he was unemployed. He quit his job some time before this period. He was gone more than he was home. Our relationship was distant. It was bad. I just didn't know how bad it was.

One day I went to talk with my neighbor, Aunt Betty. She was one of my husband's aunts. I needed someone to talk to about my marriage problems. She was someone I felt knew the Lord. I hoped she could give me some advice. That she did do. She asked me when are you going to wake up? Confused I listened as she told me "You are having so many problems because your husband is on drugs! He's not only on drugs he's selling drugs! I know you want to make your marriage work but there is only so much God requires of us. You really need to pray about your situation and decide what you are going to do about it.

I was stunned! Selling drugs! How could this be? I began to think back in my mind. Remember how he did this. He's not working. He's always gone. When he is home he sleeps all day. How could I be so naïve? Why didn't I know? We even studied this in school during our Psychiatric rotation training.

Well, to make a long story short, I confronted him about it. He admitted it was true and he made it clear if I couldn't deal with it I could leave. I tried to deal with it. I prayed for him and for our marriage but I realized he was not going to change. I had to be the one to change. That realization came the day he accused me of doing something with our TV. He said I took it or lost it or something. I didn't know what he was talking about. He was furious. He made it clear to me that he was going to kill me when he got there if I didn't tell him what happened to his TV. I found the TV in our closet. I didn't know how it got there but suspected he put it there but did not remember doing so. I also found his gun and decided that I did not want it or me to be there when he got home so I packed what I could handle with my daughter, got a ride to the bus station and dropped the gun in a trash dump on the way out of town.

I gave up. I couldn't take it any more! I was in my last semester of school but I couldn't take it any more. I quit school. It was very embarrassing and very discouraging to have gotten so far in the program and have to quit now. I did not tell Perry or Belinda or any of my classmates. I left town secretly and quietly. I went to my sister's home. When I was safe and securely out of town I called my school and explained my circumstances.

I was discouraged but my sister was very supportive. She told me not to give up. She expressed that there must be a way you can challenge the state board since you already completed so much of the program. That was something I hadn't thought of so I called the Board of Vocational Nurse & Psychiatric Technician Examiners to request an application to challenge the state board test. I completed the application and anxiously waited for a response. Weeks later the response came. In order to challenge the board the applicant must have so many hours of clinical time spent in certain areas of the hospital. I had not completed my Obstetric training therefore I did not qualify to challenge the state boards. I checked into the training programs in the area to see if I could transfer into a local program. I could but would have to take additional classes to be able to graduate from their program. Considering the hard ships I'd already faced I did not have the luxury of extended time to waste taking more classes then my original program required.

You would think that my husband would have been glad to be rid of me. He made it clear to me that he was not going to change. Well he was not. He continued to harass me. I thought I was discrete when I left town but found out when he arranged to have my daughter kidnapped in broad daylight from my sister's home that I was not discrete enough! Even after he took my daughter he continued to harass me with phone calls. I was glad to be away from him but was tormented with nightmares being away from my daughter.

After several months past I learned that I could return to school in San Bernardino. I would have to join another class that was in session but that was fine with me. Some of my relatives helped me find housing. I learned that I had a distant relative who lived in the area. She was willing to let me live with her to finish school.

I tried to focus strictly on school. It was different now because I didn't have any friends. I didn't know the teachers. The hospitals we went to were even different. I was lonely. It was hard. I cried a lot. I accused my husband of keeping my daughter from me so he began to share her with me again. He brought her over to spend the night. To my surprise he provided transportation for me to get to school. This did make my life easier. I saw a change in him so we began working on our relationship. This would later cost me big time!

One particular day I was at home alone. The phone rang. It was my older brother. Next I heard the horrible words. Mamma is dead. I froze in my tracts. Reaching for the floor I sat down. Grabbing my knees I let out a curdling cry. No! No! I think I dropped the phone. After a few moments I collected my thoughts and finished the conversation with my brother. I can't remember what else he said but soon we were headed to our hometown to attend my mother's funeral. This meant I had to miss more days from school. This concerned me but I felt I had no choice. I managed to get through another tragedy in my life. I even sang at my mother's funeral.

Talk about having obstacles. I faced challenge after challenge. Then as though I had not had enough problems, without notice or conversation my relative kicked me out. She told me if I was going to be hanging out with my husband and he was going to be hanging out around her house, he should be taking care of me. I was not sure our relationship was even going to work but now I had no place to live so he got a hotel room for us. It was nothing fancy. It was cheap. We had a bed and a bathroom.

Not surprisingly my husband resumed his old behaviors. He was gone days at a time. He left me with my small child and no transportation. I managed meals with an electric skillet and a few dishes I bought from a thrift store. I couldn't buy much because we had no refrigeration. I bought a stroller from a thrift store for a few dollars. That helped me be able to transport my daughter around on foot. I did not know how I was going to pay the rent so I went back to work as a CNA on the graveyard shift part time. Part time status was not enough to pay the room rent so I started cleaning the hotel rooms in the morning to help offset my room expenses. It was pretty apparent that most of the clientele that frequented this hotel was using the facilities for sex and partying. I would find condoms in the linen and on the floor. I thought it strange that these people did not feel any shame about leaving their used condoms for someone else to clean up. They didn't even try to hide their sin.

This was a dark time for me. I was so used to persevering and having to persevere that I didn't spend much time reflecting on my feelings. It was during this time that I realized I had a desire to one day write my life story. I remember getting a note book and trying to write my thoughts down on paper. I was struggling because things were not clear to me. It was not even clear how the present situation was going to end up. I did not have much support. I felt so alone. But I couldn't feel alone because that would not help me get to where I needed to go. I did come up with a title. It was "THE STORY OF WE". I was thinking about the things that my brothers, sister and I had gone through so I wanted to come up with a title that reflected our story. As time went on our story became my story so the title transformed into "THE STORY OF ME" my first book. That desire was forgotten almost as soon as it was birthed. I didn't have time for dreams.

We eventually moved from the hotel to an apartment. In spite of all the problems, in spite of all the obstacles, graduation day came. I was in the graduating class of 1986. We were all dressed in our blue and white uniforms. Our nursing caps looked very professional. I did not know the students in this class. But I know we shared the pride of our accomplishment. I did not have a lot of family and friends attend so again I had mixed feelings. The night was made special for me when it came time for my pinning. The director of the program called students by name and said something special about each of us. When she called me she talked about the many challenges I faced including the death of my mother. She said she was especially proud of me. No one ever said that to me before. Her words of admiration caused me to see my accomplishment in an extra special light. I must have done something special. Yes I'd done something special. Prior to hearing her words I just thought I did what I had to do. But now I new it was special too. She said not many people could have finished the program under such adverse circumstances.

Chapter 3

I passed the LVN boards with no problem. Now I had something to look forward to. I was a professional. I was no longer a butt wiper. I was already working at a facility as a CNA. I hoped I could get a job where I was already working. I submitted my application but was disappointed when the DON told me she could not offer me a job. She said my work was good but I was too quiet. I needed to learn to be more assertive. She feared that being young and soft-spoken the older staff would make it hard for me. She feared they would not respect me. So I was forced to look for employment elsewhere. I now feel this was discrimination. This discrimination may not be legally protected but is still discrimination in my books.

Even in those times nurses were in demand. In the nursing program we learned that there was a nursing shortage. I knew and still know that the medical profession is always going to be around. We are always going to have sick people. I can truly say that I've always been able to get a job. I have not always liked the jobs I got. But I could get a job.

I applied at another nursing home and was hired with no problem. Naturally I was still young and soft spoken but they didn't say anything about that. They started me on the graveyard shift. Most of the time it was easier to get a job on the midnight shift. It was called getting your foot in the door. Then when something better opened up you had a better chance of getting it. As a CNA I preferred the evening shift 3-11PM. It was not as hectic. You did not have to deal with the management staff or many families. We served dinner. By the time dinner was over and we put our patients to bed, things started slowing down. The atmosphere was usually more peaceful. Unfortunately that shift was not good for me being a new mother and having a so-called family.

The first day on the job I made a medication error. I went into a patient room to give medications. I called the patient by name, she answered. I gave her the medications. When I returned to my med cart I realized something was wrong. The name of the patient I called was supposed to be in the next bed. I had not checked the armband! How stupid of me! The rule of the "Five Rights" taught us as students to check for the right medication, the right dose, the right route, the right time and the right person by verifying the armband. This was so basic. Now I was faced with a dilemma. Do I report my error or do I pretend as though nothing happened? The patient was confused any way. That is why she responded to the wrong name. In school we were also taught that integrity was important to our success as a nurse. We would be faced with ethical decisions and would have to make our choices wisely. Besides that I was raised in the Pentecostal Church. My parents did not tolerate lying. So what did I do? At the end of my shift I went to my supervisor and told him what happened. I was nervous. I feared for my job. But he was very understanding and very encouraging. He reassured me that I was being hard enough on myself therefore he knew I would learn a valuable lesson from this and I did.

Ethic; according to Webster's New Collegiate Dictionary, ethic is the discipline dealing with what is good and bad and with moral duty and obligation. I realized almost immediately that I would face ethical decisions over and over during the course of my career.

I jumped with both feet, into learning my job. I practiced what I was taught. I applied it and I was diligent in my duties. I passed medications. I made my rounds. I did my treatments and I cared. This was a good thing but I soon learned that this was not good in every ones eyes. One night while working, one of the other nurses came to me. She was an older woman. She'd been there for a while. She was Black. She told me in no uncertain terms "We are not going to be doing all the stuff you are doing. We are not interested in working that hard so you better stop what you are doing"! She was letting me know I was making them look bad. I thought I was just doing my job. I was just following my job description. This was the second biggest and most pivotal ethical decision I faced. I was intimidated. I knew that my decision would affect my relationships at work but I also knew I had to live with my decision. This decision would shape the rest of my career. After much thought I decided I would be true to my self. I could not cheat my self or my patients by succumbing to the negative influences of others. This was the first time I dealt with Black against Black persecution related to my career.

If you aren't already familiar with this scenario I will explain it to you. Often Black people become offended if another Black person does well. They feel you are trying to be something or someone that you are not. They say you are trying to be White. So instead of supporting you and or mentoring you they persecute you. Many believe that this Black against Black persecution is a residual effect from when we as a people were in slavery. The White masters purposely pitted the slaves against each other to keep them under subjection and to keep them from opposing their true enemy.

I remember the first time I had to deal with the state surveyors. I was working the graveyard shift. They came to our facility on a complaint. I directed them to the patient room they requested. Upon entering the room they found a suction machine at the bedside. It was soiled meaning it had fluid and bodily secretions in it. I reported that I had not used the machine on my shift. They made a note of that. I was so nervous. We learned about the Department of Health Services in school. I knew they had the legal right to come to our facility any time announced or unannounced. I did not know our facility policy or procedure for responding to a surveyors visit. At the end of my shift when the DON arrived I reported what happened to him. Again he was very supportive. He even apologized to me stating, he felt bad because he was not there to support me during the visit. He knew I was inexperienced in dealing with such matters. I never knew the outcome of that complaint or what the complaint was about.

For your information the Department of Health Services also referred to, as DHS is one of the governing bodies of the health care industry. It functions on the state level of authority. There are several bodies that govern the health care industry. The first and highest authority is the Federal Government. The next is DHS. Then there are others for example Nurse Practice Acts and the Occupational Standard Hazard Act. Every facility must follow guidelines as set forth by these governing officials. If they fail to do so their actions could result in major fines or even shut down of the facility. Facilities are surveyed annually and any time there is a complaint filed against them. The results of the annual survey are public knowledge. They must be placed in a public area in the facility and be made available to any one who would inquire about them. Needless to say poor performance during a survey could effect the facilities reputation. This could affect the number of admissions they receive thus affecting their bottom line, their revenue.

I mentioned that my DON was a man a "he", but I did not say much about him. He was a young White male. I was very impressed with him. He had style. He was attractive but he presented himself as a professional and as someone who cared for his patients as well as his staff.

One night very unexpectedly Mr.***** came to the facility. He found several CNAs asleep on the job. He fired them on the spot. Then he took over completing their work until the day shift came on. Now that was impressive to me! He was a DON but he did not hesitate and he actually knew how to do the work. Even though I was new I knew this was a rarity. His example would later influence my supervisory skills and I often talked about him when I taught students of my own.

I liked working there. I didn't know it but I was making a reputation for myself. They were talking about me. I had a relative who worked there too. She was actually my in-law. One day she came to me and told me "At first I did not know why everyone was making such a big deal about you but now I see why." I was now working on day shift. She said you are doing things that other nurses don't do. Even the DON is impressed with you. She let me know my standard of work was disturbing the staff on day shift as well. One of her friends a CNA told her she did not like me asking her about her work. She felt that she already knew how to do her job and it bothered her when I asked her if she'd done this or that. I explained that being a supervisor, a charge nurse, it was part of my job to ask questions, to know what was going on and I was still learning the staff and what their capabilities were. I of course appreciated the feedback but was also puzzled. I felt I was simply doing my job. After all how do you learn accept by doing, asking and practicing what you're doing?

Work was going well but my personal life was still in the dumps! Transportation was still an issue for me. Some days I road my bike, that way I would not have to wonder whether I was or was not going to have a way to get to work. I believe my new earned income and professional status was now considered a threat to my husband. Somehow he began to realize that I could actually make it on my own. I would not need him anymore.

One morning I awakened to find another woman in my apartment. She was very casual about it. She had her daughter with her. They spent the night. I didn't even know they were in my home. For the record I will tell you she was White. She was average looking, nothing special to look at. Actually she looked rather trashy. I didn't know what was going on or why she was there but I suspected she was involved with my husband. For the record I will also tell you my husband was Black.

Normally I was and am a quiet soft- spoken individual. I was more of an introvert at that time in my life than I am now. I didn't get angry easily. But this time I was annoyed, you might say even a little bit angry! I went to work. I was working part time. All day long I thought about the events of my morning. I asked my self if I was over reacting. Maybe there is a perfectly good explanation for the whole situation. I tried to reason with my emotions, tried to make sense of the whole scene. The more I thought about it the angrier I became. I decided I was going to have some courage, put my foot down and take control of the situation! Enough was enough! I was going to kick her *** if I had too. All the way home I thought about what I was going to say and what I was going to do. When I got there, I walked into my apartment. I didn't say anything. I had beautiful crystal on my coffee table. I picked a piece of it up planning to hit her with it! My mind changed when I saw her daughter standing there in horror! I knew she did not understand what was going on. I felt compassion for her. After all I had a daughter too so I refrained from doing her bodily harm. I told this White woman very directly, I don't know why you are in my house but you better leave now! She began to cry! She pleaded with me telling me she did not understand what was going on. My husband had offered her a place to stay. She needed a place to stay because she had some serious personal problems. She didn't even know he was married or that I'd be there. I began to calm down. This was so much like my husband. I knew she was a victim in the situation just like I was. To make a long story short I got in touch with my husband. She ended up leaving that day and all was well. Not quite! You see it turned out that my husband was trying to establish a place that he could sell drugs out of. She was supposed to be his contact person, you know, run the drug house. I inadvertently messed up his plans. So he was furious! He vandalized our apartment! He broke furniture and my beautiful crystal. He blamed me for all the confusion, cursed me from A to Z and threatened to do me bodily harm! His family got involved. My family got involved. There were threats and lots of anger displayed that almost resulted in a physical altercation.

I was just trying to make a better life for my child and me. Was that too much to hope for? I just wanted to be able to take care of us because I knew I could not count on my husband for any thing. For some ungodly reason my husband did not like that. He wanted me to want what he wanted. He confessed his plan to me telling me that he was selling drugs. He wanted me to go and find us a home, any home I wanted. He would by it with drug money. We could be rich! I tried to convince him that his way was not the plan that God had for our lives. This plan would only lead to destruction and more misery. I wanted to be respected and have a job that my daughter could respect me for not participate in something degrading like living off of drugs and destroying other people's lives. I told him he was brighter than that.

He had more to offer his daughter than that. "You stupid ***** he yelled!" He was furious! He pulled lots of money out of his pockets. He told me it was thousands of dollars. He threw it on the floor in front of me. This is what you can have! I did not and would not agree with him. I chose a career instead. So he made my life a living hell. In spite of his explanations I felt he was cheating on me with this woman too. I just wanted peace.

Feeling confused and degraded I took my daughter and checked into a hotel. He'd defended her instead of me. She was not just a woman but she was a White woman, a trashy one at that. The incident stirred up feelings I'd never felt before. Yes I'd been betrayed before. Yes I'd been cheated on already but now I knew how other Black women felt when a White woman had personally wronged them. Knowing the history of Black people in America, I knew of the issues about interracial couples because of our history but never experienced this for my self. I now had to analyze my own feelings. Why did this feel worse than any other time a woman had betrayed me? Was I prejudiced against White people? No. Was I prejudiced toward this White woman? Yes. Very much so! I concluded that my insult was justified. I knew that White people had always taken from us and would continue to do so but I could not allow this incident to prejudice me against all White women or White people.

I did not have the answers to my problems. I knew my emotions were real but I still had a plan and a need to better my condition. Although my granny helped me get through school by babysitting we did not have the type of relationship that allowed me to go back home.

One day I finally decided I could not handle the pressure any more. I felt suicidal. My husband continued to harass me. One night he took my clothing; work uniforms included and threw them out the window. We lived in an upstairs apartment. It was dark out. The area where he threw my clothes was overgrown with weeds and undeveloped. I could not see where to retrieve the clothing from even if I wanted too. I was supposed to go to work the next day. I was emotionally drained. I knew if I told my husband I planned to leave him he would threaten to kill me again so I secretly slipped out of town again. This time I went to my brother's home. He was in the US Air Force. He lived on an Air Force Base so I felt that it would be a more secure environment for us. I took my daughter with me. No way was I leaving her with the maniac she called dad. I drove all night. I was scared. I kept thinking my husband would show up behind me at any minute but he did not. We made it to our destination. We arrived at Vandenberg Air Force Base in Lompoc California. The year was 1986.

Chapter 4

I was now twenty-two years of age, a single mother and a professional. I'd been through so much. It took so much effort to get to this point in my life yet I felt as though I had to do better. I needed to prove to myself that I could establish a home for my self and my child. I was tired of starting over and I was certainly tired of running.

It did not take long for me to get another job. There was only one convalescent home in town at the time. The town was Lompoc, California. I was hired on the midnight (noc) shift again. I easily settled in at work and at home.

At work I was one of three Black nurses. Remember the ratios I mentioned earlier. Laura was the Supervisor on the evening shift. She'd been there for many years. I immediately noted that Laura was respected. She was efficient and she was Black. I admired Laura. She was a supervisor but she was only an LVN. Most health care facilities required that supervisors be RNs. This was an accomplishment in itself.

My experience at this facility was not extremely eventful. I went to work and I did my job. The only mentionable event's that occurred was when I had to correct one of my CNAs for poor patient care. I previously pointed out that it was not normal by most nurse standards that I'd met, for nurses to do rounds. Well I continued to do rounds and check on my patients during my shift. I found patients who were supposed to be on Intake and Output, with extremely dry lips, soaking wet evidenced by dark brown rings of urine and or double pads underneath them. This

it was evident to me that she had not. So I asked her about these things. Because I'd tried to talk with her about her performance on several other occasions and she had not improved, I felt I should have witnesses present the next time I talked to her about the problem. After report I approached her with my concerns. She blew up! She didn't have to take this! She was leaving! As she got up to leave I advised her that that was not the answer to this problem. She could work through the situation by improving her work. She wouldn't hear me. She left. I told my supervisor what happened. She backed me up and stated she the CNA would be addressed in the morning by the DON. She sealed her own fate.

That is how it was in those days. There was a standard expected of you. It was a minimum standard. If you did not meet that standard you were called on the carpet about it. We had leaders and subordinates. Your responsibility as a leader was pretty clear. Your responsibility as a subordinate was pretty clear. I never felt that one was greater than the other. All positions were important because all were necessary. We were taught the chain of command, the organizational structure and you were expected to follow it.

Now days I find that there is very little structure in most of the facilities. No one wants to take responsibility for anything. "Leaders" spend more time trying to cover their butts or pass the buck than trying to do a good job. Or the leader is a micro manager and they stifle the growth and output of their employees. In either case you end up with substandard facilities providing substandard care and burnt out employees. No wonder there is a demand for nurses. I will dig deeper into this topic at a later time. So I will hold my thoughts for now.

Back to the CNA whom I counseled, I felt bad about the situation because I did not like confrontation but felt I had an obligation to my patients to make sure they were getting good care. I was forced to deal with the problem or deal with my conscience so I dealt with the problem.

Even though I sort of fell into the medical profession, I can say that I wanted to help people. I wanted to make a difference in the lives of the people I cared for.

The situation became known to the other CNAs causing division amongst them. Some felt and one stated to me "I like working with you" "I tried to tell them, if you just do your job, Diane won't mess with you so just do your work". The other opinion came from a young Black CNA. I called her Tira "T", "T" for trouble. She was fair skinned but felt that she was Blacker than I was. One time she told me she thought I was a dumb blond because in her opinion I acted White. That meant my mannerisms were proper and I spoke properly. Some how, I apparently lacked that certain flavor or flair that qualified me to be considered Black. She and I were good friends until this incident occurred. She felt that I'd forgotten where I came from. I was forgetting who I was. I was letting my authority go to my head. I cannot quote her because I heard this information through the grape vine. Although I tried to learn from her why she was shunning me she would not tell me herself. I learned through some of the other staff that this was how she felt.

My feelings were hurt. I thought she knew me better than that. After a while I stopped trying to mend our rift and realized her response was typical of a lot of Black people toward Blacks who are progressive. You get labeled as a sale out. This is another reason why we don't really have a peer group. Most White people tolerate you. In some cases they even acknowledge you but you never really fit in with them. Many Black people categorize you and try to hold you back.

After working at this facility for a little over a year I became bored. I knew my patients medications by heart. I knew my job well. It was no longer a challenge for me. One of the good things about this facility was it was jointly owned by the district. The district also operated an acute care hospital. Employees had the option of transferring between facilities without loosing seniority. A position opened up to work part time in the Intensive Care Unit (ICU). I got the position. This was a big step for me.

Acute care nursing is very different from long-term care nursing. The patients in long-term care were at the end of their life. They were old. In those days our mission was to take care of them until they died. In the acute care setting you take care of patients of all ages. You are not expecting them to die. The mission is to help them get well so they can go home.

I was afraid but I wanted the opportunity to grow in my field so I looked at this as an opportunity to do just that. I was now working on the evening shift 3-11PM. I was given a few days of orientation. During that time I observed another nurse in the function of her duties. Then I was assigned to work as the second nurse in the unit. The first nurse in charge was an RN. Her name was Paula. She was not friendly. She was blonde and had an attitude problem. She did her job but never gave me any instructions or offered any conversation toward me. She seemed to me as though she didn't want to be bothered with me or anyone else for that matter so I did what I knew to do and stayed out of her way.

Several months went by. It was time for my evaluation. The house supervisor called me to the Nursing office. Her name was Josie. Josie was a pretty, young Philippine

Nurse. She reviewed my evaluation with me. Overall it said I was performing at the average level. I felt this was acceptable considering the fact that I'd switched to a completely different area of expertise. But then she gave me Paula's input. Paula was the nurse I worked with in ICU. She stated that I was unmotivated; I did not anticipate the needs of my patients or the unit. Basically she was not impressed with me at all. I was stunned! I was hurt. I explained that I was afraid not unmotivated and that Paula made me feel as though I needed to stay out of her way. She was in no way supportive nor did she offer to teach me anything. I was so naïve. It never occurred to me that unmotivated is another word for lazy. And lazy is what Black people are often viewed as. I made it clear that I was willing to learn. To my relief, the house supervisor agreed with me. She told me she had observed my performance up to that point and she felt I was doing a good job. She said with time she felt I would be a very good nurse and that I needed to work on becoming more assertive. I was thankful for her input but I went home devastated.

Have you ever heard the expression Nurses eat their young? Well it is a true saying. I'm not sure if it is a woman thing or what it is but nurses are often cold and unfriendly. Instead of welcoming newcomers they throw them to the wolves and expect you to make it on your own. You sink or you swim it is your choice. Yet they always whine about being short staffed. It is double jeopardy if you are Black!

I took pride in my work. I knew I still had a lot to learn but this was very discouraging to me. I went home like a dog that had been wounded with my tail between my legs. I asked myself, what were you thinking? I should have stayed where it was safe where I knew my job well. I cried and I contemplated my future. I told my husband what happened. This was one time that he was able to advise me and he actually gave me pivotal advice. He told me Diane you have two choices. You can go back in there and fight for what you want or you can quit and leave with your tail between your legs. You said you wanted to work in the acute care setting. When you go back to work, ask questions. Force them to answer your questions and force them to notice your efforts to learn. In short don't take no for an answer. I thought about his advice and felt that he had a very good point. So I took his advice. When I went back to work I asked questions. I followed Paula around and stayed involved with what was going on. This taught me a valuable lesson. Not everyone in a leadership position is a leader. Sometimes you have to teach yourself and support yourself. I knew this lesson all to well in my personal life but now I was learning it about the work place.

I probably confused you when I stated that I talked with my husband about my problem. Well let me explain. We remained separated for some time but I decided for my daughter's sake to give him another chance. She missed her father greatly. She asked about him a lot. The big difference was that now he agreed to do things on my terms. I was now calling the shots. That was the only way I was willing to try it again. He moved to my town. He gave up his life and his negative associations. We really started over this time. I was learning to be more assertive in my personal life as well as in my professional life.

I didn't have to deal with Paula much longer. She quit anyway. I continued to learn and work in ICU.

Soon a position opened up in the Emergency Room (ER). I applied for and got that position.

Over all I'd say working in the ER was exciting! Each day presented the potential for something different to happen. I had to learn what supplies were standard for each type of presentation. We had to have things ready before the Doctor came in to see the patient. One never knew what to expect. If a patient presented with a laceration, we automatically rinsed the wound, assessed it for depth and severity and pretty much knew if it needed sutures or not. Then we set up the supplies needed for suturing. The only thing the doctor really decided was what type of suture material he wanted to use. Certain conditions automatically called for an intravenous line (IV) to be started. The Emergency Medical Technicians (EMT's) often started the IV's in the field. Complaints of a female nature went to the Obstetrics Room (OB) room. The whole concept of the ER environment was one of anticipation. It was necessary to anticipate what was coming through those doors. Unlike one of the popular series on television right now, we did not discuss our private lives and personal ambitions while caring for patients. If you stop and think about it, would you want some one taking care of you during a crisis situation to be so self-absorbed? Do you really want to know what problems they are having or what ego trip they are on or would you want them to have your best interest at heart and focus on you while you are there?

It is important to relay to you that each and every department is a specialty in itself. Each area required a different focus. They were similar in that they all required assessment skills but these skills needed to be refined and tuned to each area. ER is where I realized that one could develop intuition, a kind of insight into the condition of a patient, a feeling that something else is going on. For example a young man in his forties presents with complaints of (c/o) shortness of breath (SOB), indigestion and general malaise. He says he feels tired lately. He didn't fit the classic picture of a cardiac patient because of his age but something inside you tells you he belongs in the Cardiac Room. Something similar happened to me. I attempted to put the patient in the Cardiac Room. Judy, the director of ER intervened telling me to place them in another room but put the heart monitor leads on him. I tried to explain his symptoms. She repeated her previous directions. When the Doctor went in to see the patient he asked. "Who put this patient in this room?" The Director realizing he was upset told him the nurse did it! I of course jumped in to defend myself, don't put that on me! I tried to put him in the Cardiac Room. You told me to put him in there instead. It takes a lot of courage to stand by your own decisions and own up to your mistakes but it is the best way to learn from your mistakes. Judy was staunch. She was tall, an attractive red head. She really did know her stuff. I think she was just caught off guard that day. It really was not a big deal. But I spoke up for myself.

Over the next several years I worked in most of the departments in the hospital that a nurse could work. I went from getting my foot in the door in ICU to working in ER, Medical Surgical (Med Surg) and Obstetrics (OB)/Telemetry. At first I did not want to float to different floors. I was too green, new. But later, after I became more confident I actually liked moving around. I found that I got bored with staying in one place to long.

I was very surprised and honored one day when a day shift supervisor who worked in ICU gave me a compliment. Marilyn was a good nurse! She was old school. She was straightforward but not rude, assertive not aggressive, soft-spoken but heard. She had presence. I was nervous around Marilyn. I wanted to do a good job because she did a good job. We didn't talk much in the unit. Perhaps it was just our style. So the day that Marilyn told me she wanted to talk to me to let me know how she felt about me, my heart started pounding! We all knew that she was retiring soon. She was an attractive woman with brunette hair. She wore a bright colored lipstick. Of course she wore a white dress uniform. With her head slightly tilted forward looking over the top of her glasses she began by saying. Now that I am leaving, I can tell you what I think of you. Thump, Thump, Thump. That was the sound of my heart! She continued, I think you are a good nurse. You are very good to your patients. I listen to you when you are in the rooms with them. You are very thorough and you care. I have watched how you've grown and I am proud of you. Tears came to my eyes. I was very touched and replied, coming from you this truly is a compliment! Thank you very much! I didn't know how wise she was but realized at that moment that she'd been observing and training me in her personal way all along. She explained that she could not share those things with me before but felt she should tell me now because she was leaving. I wanted to kiss her but felt we should maintain that respectful moment. That is what I concluded. I'd gained Marilyn's respect.

Sad to say there are not many nurses like Marilyn around any more! Thank You Miss Marilyn for being an example for me and others I'm sure.

I worked for the district for a total of eight years. I transferred back and forth between the convalescent home and the acute facility several times. During that time I acquired my Director of Staff Development (DSD) certificate. One day while working at the convalescent home Jim, the administrator, approached me and asked me if I would be interested in taking the DSD class. This certificate would permit me to provide staff training and education as well as enhance my resume so I jumped at the opportunity.

Jim was very influential to me. He walked like no one else I'd known. His gait was a combination of a bounce and stride. When he was present you knew he was. He was very knowledgeable about the long- term care business. He kept things flowing smoothly in our facility. Our center was one of the top- rated nursing homes in California at the time. Lots of people talked about Jim. They complained he was too anal. He didn't like noise and chaos. He liked order. I never had a problem with him. When ever I had a problem I was always able to go to him and he helped me resolve it like the time when I discovered I'd been shortchanged on my rate of pay for almost a year.

I'd transferred back to the convalescent center. The benefits of working for the district included being able to transfer between facilities without loosing seniority or pay increases previously earned. These pay increases were called steps.

Well, one day I called HR, Human resources to ask a question about something. During the conversation, I discovered that the last time I transferred to a new position my hourly wage had been reduced. I'd lost a step. The director at the time was a personality I didn't care much for and he refused to correct the problem. He insisted there was no mistake in spite of the policy stating the contrary. I was not one to complain much or make waves but when it came to standing up for something I believed in that was another story! I went to Jim with my problem. He went over Mr. HR's head. The matter was resolved. I got substantial back pay. For this I knew Mr. HR would now not care much for me in return but I was impressed that Jim took care of business on my behalf.

Another time he came to my aide was when the nursing Director, Judy Lee came and chewed me out! I went to the job for something. She saw me in the building and approached me. She let me know that she did not appreciate my lack of participation in the events that were taking place in the facility at the time. There was an outbreak of scabies going on!

Scabies is contagious. The scabies mite is a microscopic bug that lives and breeds under the skin. It digs into and below the surface of the skin, hatches eggs and reproduces itself. The digging causes terrible itching. To rid the facility of these pestilent critters was a time consuming painstaking task. Every patient, all linens, direct care staff, their families, and families linens needed to be treated to kill the mite and stop its' spread.

I was off work when the treatment process was initiated. A co-worker and fellow classmate asked me on our way to school if I'd received the medication to treat my family and my self for the scabies. Because she asked, I went to the job to get the medication for my family. This is when Judy confronted me. She made it clear she was upset with me. I made it clear to her that I was upset because no one told me of the problem until now. I understood her concern for the facility but was upset that her concern did not include me as an employee or my family's well being. I did not receive a phone call. Nor was I asked to come in and participate in the process in any way! According to policy, when there is an emergency in the facility a phone list, a roster of the employees is to be used to notify staff of the need to come in and help or just make them aware of the problem. This had not been done. I felt that policies such as the one concerning this situation are in place for a reason. I felt singled out and I did not appreciate it. She did not back down from her opinion. Neither did I, so I went to Jim about the matter. I don't know if he said anything to her about the situation but I felt better about it just because he seemed to understand my side of things. That was the kind of leader I found him to be.

When Jim retired it was more evident that he was the glue that kept that place together. In my opinion the standard was never the same after that.

To my knowledge I was the second out of two Black DSD's in the Central Coast Area. I taught my first CNA class around 1993. Now I was the one responsible for inspiring and training someone else. I was able to give my students a foundation. Talk about coming full circle. For graduation my students presented me with red roses. I sang them a song letting them know they were the true heroes for their efforts and accomplishments in my class. It was a beautiful ceremony. Jim complimented the fact that the students blended in so well with the staff. There was not the usual us v/s them mentality. We were already a team. Later I would learn how much of a compliment that was.

Rhonda came to the graduation! Maybe it was Rhonda who brought the roses. I'm not sure. Rhonda was my buddy! She was a little older than I was. She was an LVN, a night shift creature who worked in the ER and a sister girl with a lot of personality. Rhonda pointed out to me that she wasn't sure what to think of me when she first met me. She didn't know If I was a real sister girl or not. She decided to give me a chance and we became very good friends. Rhonda was sharp. She did things fast. I did things slow. Or should I say slower than her. I remember the time she gave me a "Procrastinators Club Card." She gave it to me to make a point. We'd had a disagreement about something. The card was her way of telling me I was to slow about getting back to her. In the Black culture joking and talking about people is a past time. It is a type of sport. We used to call it capping when I was young. I don't know what people call it now. Rhonda reminded me of being with family. We laughed a lot.

Work was fun when Rhonda was around. Rhonda gave me the courage to do things I would not ordinarily do. One time we both went to a private house party. It was just a small gathering of a few guys and a few ladies. We were both scheduled to work that night but we wanted to go any way so we went. We were having a good time so we stayed longer than we should have. We kept saying we were going to leave in a few minutes. The time went by so fast. The next thing we knew, we were running through the doors' of the hospital. We ran to clock in, barely making it in time. Neither of us was dressed for work. We had our after five gear on so we had to rush and change. Of course we blamed each other for the close call. We laughed hard about this!

Another time we were talking on the phone. We were both scheduled to work that night. Neither of us felt like going in so we kind of agreed we wouldn't go in. We both called off work one right after the other. I was so afraid to call off for anything. Even when I was really sick I was afraid to call off. I had over one hundred hours of paid time off available but I was very careful about using it. Rhonda said, girl please! I'll do it if you'll do it. So we did it. Don't get me wrong. Rhonda was dedicated to her job but she was free like that. She didn't sit around and worry about things like I did.

During those years I had some positive mentors and some negative ones. I learned from their examples of how to be and how not to be. I had some good experiences and some bad ones.

I still remember my first day on the Medical Surgical floor. The nurse I was assigned to for training told me, you don't watch me. I watch you. So get started! She was supposed to show me the ropes. I was supposed to be in orientation, getting oriented to that floor. She was a White, white haired lady, an old timer. She'd worked there for many years but she was not about to share her experience with the likes of me. I think she was one of the few nurses who still wore a nurse cap. She wasn't mean but just didn't have much interest in helping anyone else. She and her white cap walked a way. I didn't see her anymore that day. I didn't know where to begin. I had medications to give, IV's to hang, patients to see, charting to do but I did not know in what order I should do those things. Somehow I made it through my shift without any lives being lost but I went home in tears that day too. Of course I wanted to quit. Then God sent help to me in the form of Pam. Pam showed me the ropes. She was an ER Nurse now supervising on the night shift. She told me how to get report, set up my IV's in advance, where things were, pass meds etc. I made notes on the information she gave me and that was all I needed to get started on the right foot.

I worked almost every floor in the hospital at one time or the other. I took care of those with problems ranging from A-Z. Some of these highlights include the time one of our church mothers, Mother **** presented to the ER by ambulance.

In my denomination church mothers were the elderly women who were spiritual and wise. They were respected for their ability to love and council the younger women and saints. They lived Holy and were able to get a prayer through to God. By this I mean when they prayed they got answers to their prayers.

I didn't recognize her at first. Her complexion was darker than normal, her face swollen and she was unresponsive. I was on the code team.

When a code is called that means it is a life- threatening emergency. Some one needed help and they needed it now or they may not live. The code was called throughout the hospital. Code Blue STAT to ER! Code Blue STAT to ER! The ER doctor, nurses, lab techs, respiratory techs and x-ray tech all came out of the woodwork. They were there in seconds, me included. We worked fervently on her to revive her to no avail. Minutes seemed like hours. The room became a mess.

Supplies were everywhere. After much effort the doctor called the code off and pronounced the official time of death. It was only after the code, when he said her name; I realized she was someone I knew. The name echoed in my head as if to help me process what I just heard him say. I then leaned over her lifeless body to look into her face. It did not look like her but it was her. The room was quiet now. No more hustle and bustle. I thought about her husband, concerned about how he was going to feel. I remembered how kind she'd been to me and remembered the special gifts she'd given me for no special reason. It was more than I could contain. I was supposed to return to my floor, the Med Surg floor after the code but I needed a moment to compose myself. I needed to be alone. I went first out into the hallway and then outside to the parking lot. Once I was safely alone I let the tears flow.

Incoming vehicle accident! Incoming vehicle accident! The EMT gave the information about the person we were about to receive. It was bad. Seconds later the doors burst opened and the ambulance brought in the victim of a vehicle accident. In an effort to conceal the identity of the patient involved I will just say they were in bad shape. Massive trauma occurred to the body almost splitting them in two. Still alert and moaning the victim held on to life. Again the code team worked frantically to save our patient. Again I was part of the team. I don't remember if I was working in ER that day or if I was just on the code team. I helped to start one of the IV's. In a situation like this you put in as many lines as you can because of the massive loss of blood. The IV fluid is necessary to prevent shock. During shock the heart rate speeds up and the blood pressure drops. If these symptoms continue loss of life is eminent. The IV fluid replaces the fluid loss to help maintain blood volume. It was apparent that our patient needed surgical intervention to repair the damage he'd incurred if he was going to make it. Everyone did his or her part. The OR, Operating crew, was called in and within minutes we transported the patient to surgery. I remember praying for the patient and his family. I also remember feeling proud because I'd never seen such an efficient team of workers as I'd seen that day and I was proud to be a part of that team. Later we learned that the patient pulled through! I knew God was with him.

Another high light of working in the ER was getting to work with DR. Smell good. Dr. Smell good was not his real name. Several of the nurses including myself loved the way he smelled. He wore very nice cologne. I still remember the name, Halston Z-14. To make a long story short, we never knew anything about him. When we had time we made up reasons to go see him in the ER. It was Rhonda who made this name stick.

Dr. Zem for short, was another reason I enjoyed working in the ER. Dr. Zem was tall and in my opinion exotic. I don't remember his nationality but do remember he had pretty curly brown hair and pretty green eyes. He seemed to be shy and I enjoyed semi flirting with him.

We actually had a great team of Doctors in our facility. All were at minimum competent. Some were very good. Very good for me included a pleasant bedside manner. Others were excellent!

Dr. S**** was a Black surgeon. Initially I was very intimidated by Dr. *****. He was small in stature but his mannerism commanded respect. He was pleasant to his patients but curt with the staff. I later grew to respect this Dr. more than most Drs. I'd ever worked with. He was efficient; skilled and printed the most legible Dr's orders I've ever seen even to this day. As I became more experienced I realized he wanted things done right. One day I complimented him for his legibly printed orders. He explained to me that he made it a point to print clearly to prevent errors from occurring when caring for his patients. He felt that the lack of care and taking time to write clearly lead to unnecessary errors and caused the staff to have to call him to clarify his instructions also unnecessarily. I translated that to mean, if we take the time to do things right the first time, we won't have to waste time going back to do it again. His orders were clear and detailed. His patients did not develop postoperative infections. I also concluded that he cared about his patients and took pride in the quality of his work. I related well to that. Later he began to offer to show me new procedures and explain things to me. I never told him how much he inspired me to be a better nurse. I was again impressed by the fact that he was a Black man. I have not since worked with another Black surgeon, male or female, competent or otherwise.

Most of my experiences up to this point were positive ones. I did not give much thought to such things as racial prejudice. There were three incidents during my LVN years that I can recall that my race may have been significant. The first one was the incident with Paula I mentioned earlier in my story. The next occurred one day while working on the telemetry unit.

Our telemetry unit was adjacent to our ICU and OB units. This day I was assigned to work telemetry. This is a unit where patients with cardiac related or cardiac problems were monitored. Often they had other diagnosis as well such as Diabetes, CVA (Cerebral Vascular Accident and Confusion. I had a full load. My patients were needy. They had IV meds to be hung, finger sticks to be done, meds to be given to name a few things. I began to feel overwhelmed. I called the supervisor to ask for help. Agnes was her name. She was Phillipino. Agnes had always been good to me. I had confidence in her abilities as a nurse and a supervisor. On this day she surprised and disappointed me.

She went to my co-workers to ask them to help me. They were the two nurses that were assigned to OB that day. There were two of them. They had two or three patients' total. Their unit was very quiet. So much so that both of them were sitting in the nurses lounge reading magazines. According to Agnes they told her they did not see why I needed help because they'd seen me talking on the phone a few times. I explained to Agnes that my daughter was sick. My husband called to check with me about her status a few times because he was going to take her to be seen by her doctor. That was the end of that. My co-workers continued to read their magazines. I continued to run ragged the rest of my shift. Agnes did not insist that either of them help me.

OB nurses were commonly referred to as premadonas. Their staffing ratios were better than most floors. Compared to other floors OB nurses were slow most of the time. The patients were much more independent. Of course that was a good reason to work OB but I did not see it as a reason to leave a fellow nurse or patients hanging. I was furious! That memory stayed with me for a long time. To this day I don't understand why Agnes did not back me up! One of the nurses was White, the other Hispanic. For some reason neither of them felt I needed help.

It is because of situations like these that Blacks feel we must always be better than our co-worker counter parts. I could never get away with sitting and reading while another co-worker is being overwhelmed, nor would I want to. I would later learn that this was nothing compared to the other racial bias and double standards I would endure and be held to.

The only other time I was confronted with the race issues was when Zena came to me with a concern. Zena was the supervisor on MedSurg. She was from Trinidad. She was loud and animated but cool. She was to the point about most things. This was her way. I liked Zena. This day she asked to speak to me because she was investigating why an admission assessment was not done on a patient of mine.

Technically LVN's were not allowed to complete admission assessments for patient records. The assessment was considered to be an RN responsibility. The way the hospital got around this technicality was to have the LVN do most of the assessment or all of it; CNAs could fill in the vital signs and have the RN on duty sign or co-sign the assessment.

On this night the RN on duty was a Black nurse named Joy. I'd done all of the assessment that I could do. I left it at the patient's bedside and asked Joy to complete her part. She assured me she would. The night continued. Upon returning to the room later I found that the assessment was still not done. I reminded Joy about it. After several times I decided I'd done what I could do about the situation and left it up to Joy to complete it. It never got done. Now Zena was asking me why.

Joy had a different version of the story. She blamed it on me. Zena called us into the office together and I continued to stand behind my story. I can't remember If Joy ever fessed up to her part in the incident but it was during this time that Zena told us she felt it was ashamed that we were not helping each other more. We were two of very few Blacks in the nursing profession. According to her it was very common to see other races back each other but not that common to see Blacks support each other. I would not get the chance to see if that was a reality because after my years as an LVN I didn't work with many other blacks.

I was usually the only Black person or one out of two in a whole facility. Because we traveled growing up and I was exposed to different cultures this didn't bother me much.

That was not the case at this hospital. Over the years we represented our hospital with a number proportioned to our number in the community.

It did bother me when people asked me if I was a CNA when they first saw me at the hospital. I wondered why they never asked, "Are you an LVN or an RN? Was it because they did not expect me as a Black person to be a professional? I was not sure. I think that was the first time I wondered how others perceived me in my profession being a Black nurse.

Chapter 5

My life was changing in major ways. After 13 years my marriage finally came to an end. I knew I needed to make some changes in order to be able to sustain myself financially. I had been taking classes toward my RN prerequisites and was seeking placement at the local colleges to enter the RN program. I was accepted into Santa Barbara City College.

I filed for a divorce, relocated to a near by city, started a new job and started the RN program all within months of each other. This was not just a terrible time in my life. It proved to be the darkest yet most pivotal time in my life. My life was both in a downward spiral and I was being advanced at the same time. During this time I came to the end of me, rejected me, and then came to understand me better than ever.

I tell about the challenges of my childhood and my marriage in great detail in my biography so I won't tell them again in this story.

Santa Barbara is a wealthy tourist town in Central California. It is home for many celebrities and people of influence. The culture is laid back but snobby. The emphasis is on physical beauty but the people are indifferent and detached. It has many attractions including beautiful beaches and Restaurants.

Santa Barbara City College's RN program was considered to be one of the best in the state. The grading scale was higher. What was normally a B average in other schools was a C at SBCC. They offered a self-paced program. You were encouraged to keep up with the rest of the students but classes started at different times and it was up to you as the student to request to start each module when you were ready for it. Because I was an LVN I only needed 30 more units to qualify me to become an RN.

For the most part school itself was not hard for me. The most difficult part of going back to school was actually being an experienced nurse but having to act like a novice. I knew from my first experience in nursing school that school only scratched the surface of nursing and merely introduced you to the medical field. Now I'd been working in the real world but was being treated as though I shouldn't and didn't know anything. This was not the case with all of my instructors. Most of them were cool. As with most memories we have, it only takes one bad experience to cast a negative light on the whole experience. Combined with everything else that was taking place in my life during this time, Evan became my bad experience.

Similar to my LVN program experience, I gained a few buddies at the start of the program. There were four of us. Kim and An became my closest comrades. Kim was White. She was a single mother like me. An was single and Asian. Kim and I were both working and struggling to raise our daughters while going to school. An came from a well off family. He worked off and on but he didn't really have to. We got together for lunch, research or lab when we could. The Lab was where we practiced our clinical skills before we were able to perform them in the hospital. We shared our problems with each other. We talked about our love life and lack of love issues, as well as other challenges we faced in the program. They were my support system throughout school. If it were not for them school would have been next to impossible for me to endure.

This time I had no family support. One of my best friends shared her family with me. They became my family. She helped watch my daughter for me. Our daughters were friends from Kindergarten. When I was not working or in school I was at Homie's house. Homie was Japanese and White. I believe the Lord placed Homie in my life at this time because I was so lonely and times were so rough. Thank you Homie, for being my friend.

I worked twelve-hour shifts on the telemetry floor at a big hospital in Santa Barbara. I hated almost every minute of that experience. I came from a sixty-bed hospital to a four hundred plus bed hospital. I felt alone. Santa Barbarans were not known for their warmth or friendly nature. I was again one of two or three blacks now in a much larger setting. We worked long hours with very little time for breaks. Sometimes all I got was a thirty- minute break. Thirty minutes is not nearly enough time to regroup or refresh yourself if you are working a twelve- hour shift.

Shortly after starting my new job I was floated from the telemetry floor to the orthopedic floor. I did not know I was going to be floated when I was hired. I barely had my bearings on my assigned floor therefore I was not comfortable going to another floor. I called the supervisor to tell her my concern. She asked me are you refusing to go where you are being assigned to work. I knew by her tone of voice that she was threatening me to go where assigned or face the consequences. I needed my job so I went. I didn't know where supplies were. No one offered to show me around or help me. I was so far behind. When I finally got a break I went in the break room and cried.

Learning to read the telemetry strips was difficult for me. I had to take the test several times before I passed it. My supervisor was cool about it though she assured me I would pick it up and I did.

I learned much more about laboratory values and the importance of monitoring them on the tely unit. Sodium and Potassium levels were especially important. I developed my own color-coded system for keeping track of labs I received in report when I came on duty as well as any labs obtained during my shift. All other significant changes were included. I wrote in one color when I received report. I wrote in another color when I added something to my report. I circled things when they were especially significant etc. etc.

To my surprise, we encouraged our patients to get out of bed and walk within the first day of being transferred to our floor. Many of our patients were post-operative from open- heart surgery. We referred to them as cabbages (CABG). CABG stands for Coronary Artery Bypass Graft. A CABG is a surgical procedure done to reestablish or improve blood flow to the heart. Many of our patients were in there seventies and eighties. I was fascinated that they were able to move much less walk after such a procedure. I felt great compassion for them. They looked like they'd been butchered. The procedure left them with a long vertical chest incision and a long vertical incision on the inner aspect of their lower leg. Sometimes they had an incision on each leg; sometimes the incisions were long enough to reach their thigh. The wounds were often red and angry looking. Sometimes they were weeping and oozing serous drainage. One of the primary focuses's for me as a nurse was pain management. It was imperative that we maintained a comfort level sufficient enough to promote mobility. Walking prevented other complications such as blood clots or post- operative pneumonia.

I really came to appreciate what they'd been through when I was able to observe an open-heart surgery as a student. This was a requirement. For me this was probably the highlight of the RN program.

I was nervous because I didn't know if I could handle what I was about to see. We scrubbed and sanitized our selves per hospital protocol. We were directed to stand in a specific place so we could see but not be in the way. We were reminded to breathe so we did not pass out from lack of oxygen due to holding our breath, something you do without thinking about it when you are nervous.

There were several teams present in the OR. The total team consisted of several surgeons, several nurses, technicians and the anesthesiologist. The cardiac surgeon worked over the chest of the patient. The second surgeon worked on removing the veins from the lower extremities that would be used as the new grafts to the heart. The procedure literally involved cutting the chest open and keeping it open with massive clamps. It reminded me of times when I cut and cleaned a whole chicken to prepare it for a meal. I was fascinated to know that the team literally kept the patient alive by causing the patient's blood flow to circulate via a Cardiopulmonary Bypass Machine (CPB). The CPB oxygenates and circulates the blood flow bypassing the heart so that the heart can be stopped. The blood leaves the body, goes thru the CPB machine and is returned to the body. Then the surgeon can work on the heart without interference of blood flow or movement. The surgeons worked simultaneously to keep from losing time. They want to minimize the amount of time the patient spends under anesthesia literally suspended between life and death. New blood vessels are attached to the heart in the areas needed. The vessels were taken from the veins in the legs. When the surgery is complete the heart is stimulated by fibrillation, the blood flow rerouted back through the heart and hopefully all is well.

It was during the observation of this surgery that I gained a new appreciation for the intricacies of the human body. It was impossible for me to believe that a fine specimen such as this could evolve in and of itself. I knew in my spirit there is a God. Now I had a greater appreciation for his wisdom and creativity.

For the most part I was doing the same kind of work as a student that I did as an LVN in the real world. The major difference was now I had to give IV medications. As an LVN we could hang IVs with fluid such as .45%Saline, Saline or D5W (5%Dextrose and water), LR (Lactated Ringers solution), TPN (Total Parenteral Nutrition), Multivitamin solutions (MVI), Potassium solutions and Lipids. We even gave blood. I was already IV certified so I'd been starting and monitoring IV's for years now. It was a challenge to learn to use different IV tubing and different IV machines because I worked for one hospital for so long. Now I had to hang IV antibiotics and give medications intravenously as well as intramuscularly and subcutaneously. That included giving meds thru Central Venous Lines and caring for Central Lines. Central lines are intravenous lines inserted into the Subclavian vein. They are in close proximity to the heart and can pose a risk for infection to the patient if not cared for properly. Generally they, dressings are changed every two to three days using sterile techniques depending on your facilities policy. This new responsibility frightened me.

The harder part of getting thru the program was keeping my focus. My personal life was in turmoil. My husband fought against my petition for divorce most of the time I was in school. My credit was now ruined. Bill collectors were calling me day and night. I was in the midst of a terrible divorce and going thru the rejection of a rebound relationship that ended viciously. Some nights I couldn't sleep. Some days I hit bottom emotionally and all I wanted to do was sleep. Thank God for hot baths, being able to go dancing on the weekends and a counselor. My job offered a support program to its employees. For the first time in my life I knew I needed help if I was to make it thru this very difficult time in my life.

I remember going to school one day. I didn't want to go but I had to attend a particular lecture in order to stay on track in the module that I was in. We had to complete certain theory classes before we could do the labs or move in to the clinical setting for that module. I remember walking to my class but I could see myself walking. It felt as though I was outside of myself watching myself. I went to class. I sat in class but could not tell you what the teacher lectured about except I do remember discussing the symptoms of Appendicitis. The teacher was telling a story about a patient who almost died because the doctor did not identify her symptoms to be those of Appendicitis. Rebound tenderness in the right lower abdomen is a classic symptom of Appendicitis. I remember thinking it odd that the doctor she was talking about did not know that. After class the teacher came to me to ask if I was ok. I remember telling her I was not ok. She confirmed that she could tell by looking at me that I was not ok. She suggested that I take a break from school. I told her I did not have the luxury to take a break. I believed that school would not be any easier for me later on. My finances would not improve until I completed the program and I got a better paying job. I was the only breadwinner in my life so I felt that I had no choice but to push myself beyond my normal capacity.

The buck stopped with me! I was it! I knew my daughter was depending on me.

The first semester of school I worked twelve- hour shifts, full time hours, trying to maintain my bills. My ex husband refused to pay child support or help pay any of the debt we acquired during our marriage. I began to feel guilty because I didn't see my daughter much. She was ten at the time and I knew she was also hurting because of the divorce so I decided to reduce my hours at work so I could have a little bit more time with her. I knew my credit would suffer if I did not keep up my bills but I knew my daughter was suffering now and I didn't want her to suffer any more than she had to so I made the decision to cut back my work hours.

Most of my teachers were easy to please. I did what was required of me and I moved through each module without incident. I even received compliments from several teachers.

We did our clinical at several hospital sites. While at St Francis, I did have a minor problem, one day when I had to demonstrate a bed bath. Instead of doing it exactly by the book, I improvised. I made a basin of warm to hot water. I placed several wash clothes in it so I would not have to use the same cloth on any unwashed area once my cloth was contaminated. It was especially important that you did this when cleaning areas such as the face and genitals. Naturally you weren't supposed to wash the face with the same cloth used to wash the genitals. When I finished using each cloth I placed it to the side in my soiled area and proceeded to get a new cloth. I worked from head to toe, right to left, genitals front to back, saving the back and buttocks for last. I paid special attention to the feet. As I stated earlier cleaning between the toes was a pet peeve of mine. I carefully covered the mattress to protect the bedding from water that may drip from my washcloth and covered each area of her body after washing it only exposing her when necessary. I made sure the water temperature remained hot enough by checking with the patient. She assured me it was. Finally I applied lotion to her skin. Even this was done with special attention. I warmed the lotion first by rubbing it between my hands prior to applying it. When I completed the bath I assisted her in putting on a new gown, cleaned up my mess and made sure she was comfortable before I left. My patient thanked me and complimented my work. I thought all was well. I continued my assignment for the day. At the end of the day my instructor called me to conference with her. This was routine. She was very complimentary. She told me how meticulously I'd performed the procedure assigned to me. But there was one problem! I did not change my water between washing her genitals and washing her back and buttocks. I argued that I did not need to change my water because I never placed the contaminated washcloth in my basin. And I used a clean washcloth to clean her back and buttocks. In spite of my rational, my instructor told me I would not be signed off for completing a bed bath that day. I immediately became worried. I thought she was going to write me up or put me on warning. She quickly alleviated my fears. Oh, no, you will just have to repeat the procedure tomorrow she said. I was so relieved. When the time came to repeat the procedure I did it exactly by the book and she signed me off. It was this type of standard that I was held to during my training as an RN student.

I did not see the need for such perfection. The most important point in my opinion was that the patient was made clean and comfortable without cross contamination. There is the potential for patients to acquire infections while in the hospital due to cross contamination or simply because their immune system is compromised from being sick if we as nurses are not careful during our provision of care for them.

But I trusted this teacher's judgment. In my opinion she was articulate, refined and carried herself well. She presented herself to be knowledgeable, as a professional and she was Black. She had a distinguished look about her. She had just a touch of grey in her hair. Her complexion was smooth. I cannot recall her name but I remember her very well. She'd observed my clinical skills on several other occasions and seemed to be pleased with my performance. The only other correction I recall she offered me was the day after I called in sick. I reported to clinical the next day and I should have called her first to let her know I was coming in. In the real world, when you call off it had to be done daily. You were expected to show up the next day unless you specifically called to say you were not coming in. Again, I was thinking like a real nurse not a student. I understood her point and was very relieved when she continued to work with me. She further explained that they were not there as instructors to give us a hard time but to teach us and to make sure we got things right.

Well I had another teacher who did not have this same philosophy. She seemed rather to enjoy making students nervous and giving them a hard time. Because of her I was leery and thought that I could be disciplined for any little mistake. Evan's reputation preceded her. Most students said Evan was so heaven. Most of those students were White of course. In the class that started with us there were two other Blacks beside myself. Evan found problems with both of those students. Both of them reportedly discontinued the program for some reason and it was rumored that Evan was the cause of their trouble. Naturally this put me on edge. So when I was assigned to Evan I made it a point to know my stuff but I found out that was not enough even for me.

One day Evan assigned me to put a catheter in a female patient. A catheter is a tube inserted into the Urethra (the place that urine comes from) to collect urine. Sometimes the doctor orders them to be placed to stay in for a time other times they are ordered to be put in and taken right out. I think this one was ordered to stay in. I gathered all my supplies and called my instructor Evan. I'd done so many catheters by this stage in my career that I was not worried about the procedure. I'd cathed males and females both young and old. I was worried about having to do it for Evan. I explained the procedure to my patient after introducing myself. I set up my supplies. Evan insisted that I elevate the patients head semi fowlers, a term meaning, little higher than flat but less than sitting straight up. From experience I knew this was not good because this position reduced visibility of the Urethra and compressed the areas between the Urethra, Vagina and the Anus closer to each other but she was the instructor so I had to do it her way. The Urethra is the top opening of the three. That is the landmark. I draped and prepped her and began to insert the catheter tip into her Urethra. I did not get any urine back right away so I pulled back a little and reinserted the tubing. Still, there was no urine. Evan became nervous! She asked where is your flashlight? Knowing the female anatomy I knew I was in the right place so I assured her I did not need a flashlight. I pulled back and reinserted the tubing again and wallah! I got a backflow of urine. I was actually frustrated with Evan because she made everything more difficult. In the real world I learned from experience not to elevate my patient's head especially if she is female, some times you may not get urine right away and we rarely if ever use flashlights to get the job done. Afterwards she let me know I was "lucky" because she would have had to write me up if my technique had not worked. It was her technique that complicated things in the first place! Later that day during post conference she conveyed my successful procedure to the class and confessed I'd done it like a professional stating she'd always had problems inserting catheters and found it necessary to use a gooseneck flashlight to be able to see. You'd think I would have felt better after she confessed this to the class. Well I didn't. Instead this let me know that some of the students were experiencing problems with her because of her lack of experience not the other way around. But the students paid the price for it. And they just happened to be Black. I did not trust her after that. I knew she would be watching me more closely.

I was right. On two separate occasions after this Evan wrote me up. The first situation occurred when I had to hang an IV antibiotic. I gathered my supplies as usual and called Evan. I identified myself, the patient; the correct medication etc. etc. I hung the medication. I set it to drip at the ordered rate. When we left the room Evan let me know I'd forgot something. I forgot to mix the medication. I was used to hanging IV's but this bag was different. A portion of the bag had to be pushed in to release the medication into the solution. Then you mixed it by shaking it a few times. It was ready to be hung. I forgot to mix it. In Evans mind this was equivalent to missing a medication. I understood her thinking but felt that a simple reminder about the use of the special bag would have served me just as well. I was a diligent and tentative student. I always went back to check on my patients and would have figured out that something was wrong when I checked on the bag. She chose to write me up instead.

The second occasion occurred when the nurse I was assigned to work with that day, asked me to go with her to do a dressing change. I informed her several times that I could not do the dressing change without my instructor. I called Evan several times. That was the procedure. We had to have an instructor with us when doing special procedures until we were signed off. Then we could do them independently. We waited and waited. The nurse told me I could do it with her. She'd be right there with me. It was no problem. I gave in and went with the nurse to change the dressing. Evan came into the room before we finished. Again she wrote me up. She informed me that no matter what any one else says I was to follow her instructions as a teacher not the nurse. There were liability issues. My behavior was not excusable. When I told the nurse she got me in trouble she talked to Evan on my behalf but Evan reassured her that it was not her fault. She told her she'd had other issues with me. That's why she wrote me up.

Now I knew I had to be perfect. There was no leeway for me where Evan was concerned. Now mind you I saw other students come to class unprepared and forget supplies or forget to do things. That was ok though. They just gave some excuse or apologized and they were excused. This was when I began to feel like being Black was a strike against me. I had to be better than the other students to make it. Evan did not give me the benefit of the doubt like she did the other White or minority students. Her compliments were always laced with suspicion. It seemed she did not give my fellow Black students the same consideration as the other students either because they were either suspended or stressed out by her. I later learned that one student did re-enter the program and made it through the next time. She was one of the LVN's that started with me.

I strived for perfection after these occurrences. I made it to Complex Care. Complex Care was the final phase of the program. During Complex Care you were assigned more patients. Usually we had only two patients each clinical day. Now I would be assigned four. I chose to do my Complex Care rotation on the Telemetry floor where I worked. I felt this would give me an advantage, something I greatly needed.

I looked forward to getting out from under the scrutinizing eye of "so heaven" Evan. During Complex Care each student was to be observed and evaluated by their peers not the instructor. The student was assigned so many of the nurse's patients. The nurse completed the student evaluation at the end of the shift. Most of the nurses knew me by then. I thought all I had to do was do a good job. Not so. Each day at the beginning of my shift Evan came to listen to my report. She made it clear that she wanted to continue to watch me when I did procedures such as give shots or IV meds even though I'd already been signed off on all the required skills. She came to listen to my reports at the end of the shift and she refused to look at the evaluations given to me by my peers. Every single evaluation that I received was above average, excellent. My coworkers told me I should be training them because they knew I was a real nurse already and I was a good nurse. This went on every day. I kept my peer reviews in spite of the fact that Evan would not read or accept them. I did not know if she would make up something to get rid of me. All she needed was one more thing against me. She continued to listen in on my reports, even paid me another compliment as though she was surprised telling me she'd never seen a report sheet system like mine. It was unique. Explain it to me, she requested. I did. But I continued to distrust her. At the end of Complex Care I was sure I'd get an A. All of my evaluations were excellent. What else could I get?

The day came for finals. Most students took one or two finals each day until they were all completed. I was down to the wire. I had to take three or four finals in one day. Between working, mothering and studies, things just worked out that way. I was up almost the whole night before reading and cramming. My brain was like jelly. I had no idea what I was going to or would not remember for each test. I could not afford to fail one final. That would mean I had to return next semester to retake it or retake the module. I was determined I would not, could not suffer through that type of agony any longer. I took each test one by one. My brain was in overload but I persevered. Afterward, the instructor giving the test told me she didn't know how I did it. Most students struggle through one or two. You did three or four. I told her I did what I had to do. I did not have family to help pay for my schooling. In short I did not have the luxury of failing!

I knew Evan had it out for me but I felt it was better to put up with it then to speak up for my self. I was to close to the finish line to allow anything to mess things up for me now so I held my piece. When I learned that I passed all of my finals I felt safe enough to complain about Evans harassment of me. I complained to my counselor who also held a position of authority at the college and I showed her my evaluations. Evan had only given me a B. She justified this by saying I was late to class a few times. Interesting, she never talked to me about being late although I was late a few times because I had to drive an hour to school. She explained she wouldn't take my peer evaluations because she didn't need to see them. She already knew what was going on concerning my performance. After I complained she reviewed my evaluations and changed my grade. I was satisfied just knowing she was in the wrong and that I'd passed. I told her that was enough for me. I did not want special treatment. I only wanted what I deserved. I didn't even check to see what she changed my grade to. I was just glad to be out of there.

I hated almost every minute of living near Santa Barbara. Santa Barbarians in my opinion were not warm or friendly people. I hated working at this hospital. Everything was a struggle. Before I finished school I'd already moved back to Lompoc. Lompoc was home for me. I was glad to be home.

I graduated with my class this time. Graduation was not that special for me. I felt I deserved more than a graduation ceremony. I deserved to celebrate! Celebrate I did. I threw a party complete with food, champagne and a DJ.

Chapter 6

Before I graduated I quit my job in Santa Barbara. I hated working there. I hated living there. I wanted that feeling of home again. I wanted to be at home so I found a job closer to home. I moved back to Lompoc. Ironically I returned to the very apartment complex that I'd lived in with my husband prior to my divorce.

Creditors were still hounding me. My husband was now my ex-husband. I was fearful that he would one day find me and end my life but things were not quite as gloomy as they had been. I did have new hope for the future.

I had a nice Town Home. I managed to keep my car and a few of my credit card accounts. I had a new job in Santa Maria.

I was still an LVN because I was waiting to take my state board test. While waiting for my state board results I worked as an RN through an interim permit. I liked my new job. I liked the staff. It was a small place a fifty-nine-bed nursing home ran by a husband and wife team. It was not state of the art in appearance, nothing fancy. But it was cozy and cute. I felt like the staff cared for each other and for the residents.

One of the things that really impressed me about this place was the fact that the staff consisted of several cultures. There were Whites, Philippine's, Hispanics and myself the Black nurse but I did not feel singled out. I did not feel alone.

I remember thinking how some of the staff did not dress professionally, their uniforms sometimes were unkempt. Some wore short pants to work. I'd never seen that before. Initially I was skeptical of what I saw but I kept an open mind and was pleased to find that when the chips were down these were people I could count on.

It was now 1996. This year the State Board test changed from a paper test to the computerized NCLEX (National Council Licensure Examination for Registered Nurses). The state board test was normally several pages long. The computerized test now had a maximum of 200 plus questions and a minimum of sixty-five questions, give or take a few. It was set up so you had to answer a certain percentage correctly. If you reached that amount early the test automatically ended. However if you missed a certain percentage it also shut off automatically. If you answered so many correct and so many wrong it may also continue to give you questions for several hours so you could leave the testing site really unsure of how well you did. My memory is not certain but I only answered between sixty to eighty something questions and the computer excused me. Needless to say I was afraid to open my test results when they came. I swallowed hard, opened the envelope and read, Diane Shanell Mixon, an applicant for licensure by the California Board of Registered Nursing, Has PASSED the National Council Licensure Examination for Registered Nurses. I was at the mailbox when I read the news. I couldn't even wait till I got inside to open my mail. Talk about relief and joy! All my hard work, pain and suffering paid off.

Ken was the DON. He was an elderly White man close to retirement age. He wore a long white lab jacket signifying he was from the old school. This comforted me. Each day he made his daily walk through the halls to see what was going on.

A few of the highlights I recall from this experience include the Holiday Season. I felt special when the owners, the husband and wife team blessed us each with gifts of Poinsettias and a gift certificate for a turkey. Being a new single mom every little bit helped. The feeling of family was there.

There were times when I worked the evening shift that I did not have a sitter for my daughter so I took her to work with me. The staff enjoyed her company. They helped to entertain her. She played the piano. They even played and hula hooped with her. No one ever complained or gave me a hard time about bringing my daughter to work with me.

It was here that my love for Philippine food was solidified. Several of the nurses were Philippine. They invited me to their homes for birthday parties and often brought food from their culture to our potlucks. Some of my favorites were Lumpia, Pancit and Chicken Adobo.

One evening while working as a charge nurse, one of our residents arrested. His heart stopped. He was fine earlier in the shift but was found in his bed still warm but not responding. The CNAs responded expertly. Within minutes we were performing CPR as a team. This time I did the chest compressions. Some one else bagged him (gave him oxygen via an Ambu bag). When the paramedics arrived they complimented our performance and the effectiveness of the chest compressions being given. They were able to tell how well we were doing by the reading from the cardiac monitor. He did not make it but I remember thinking, if that were me as a patient, I'd want this team there for me. At that moment it did not matter how they dressed. They took care of business!

I enjoyed my time at that facility. The only reason I did not stay long was because they did not offer benefits that suited my needs as a single mother and I ended up on the night shift. From past experience I knew that would not last long. I was simply not a night shift creature.

When I told Ken I was leaving to work in an Urgent Care. He told me I would not like it. .

Chapter 7

My need for better hours and benefits lead me back to Santa Barbara. I decided to try something new. One thing I knew about myself. I was not afraid to try new things. Now that I was an RN I wanted to explore new areas.

I was hired to work in an urgent care clinic. Even though it was called Urgent Care, I had the impression I would be working in a doctor office type setting. There were some similarities. For the most part, it was too much like working in the ER. When I was younger I liked the excitement of the ER. Now ten years older and recovering from the trauma of my divorce, I had no desire for traumatic situations and believe me caring for a patient needing immediate cardiac intervention without any assistance is traumatic. Try starting an IV, doing an EKG, giving emergency medications and O2, monitoring, documenting and calling the ambulance by your self. Even with experience this was anxiety producing for me. I decided this was not for me either.

Ken was right. He said I was more of a hands' on, interactive person. I enjoyed getting to know people. This environment did not provide that for me.

I was again the only Black nurse in my department. The environment included Whites and Hispanics but it was not warm or embracing.

When I say embracing, I am referring to the ability to reach out and connect to people out side of ones own culture. I'm talking about establishing some common ground.

Chapter 8

I decided to try the acute care setting again. I found a job back in Santa Maria. I would now be working on the OB/GYN floor as an RN.

Santa Maria was located about 40 minutes north of Lompoc, California. Lompoc was an hour north of Santa Barbara. Both are located centrally along the coastline. The weather is usually nice. The temperature in the summer months usually stays between seventy and eighty. The nights often cooled to the 50's. The unique thing about Lompoc was the changes in the weather in the course of one day. Waking up it may be chilly but by mid- morning the sun may come out. By after noon the wind may be blowing and by evening it is actually cold. It's rarely really cold or really hot there.

One of the things I came to enjoy when I commuted was the beautiful scenery. On the way to Santa Maria was agriculture, mountains and pastures. The drive was never that bad.

I'd like to say I found my nitch in Santa Maria. That was not the case. I worked at a medical center for a short period. My memories of that time were neither bad nor good. They were typical. By this time it was clear to me that the reasons for my feelings of burn out when I was an LVN were the same reasons for my frustrations now.

I continued to desire to care for my patients but found it increasingly difficult to do so.

Several years before, the concept of DRG's (Diagnostic Related Groups), were introduced to the medical profession. Hospital Boards and Administrators now felt it necessary to standardize care. Diagnoses pertaining to specific groups were lumped into a category. Theoretically each category should require so much money to treat those kinds of conditions. If it was costing more, someone was going to have to answer to someone. This was the beginning of the decline in the provision of good health care in my opinion. Now the amount of time it took to provide care was computed by dollars and cents. No more being thorough. No more getting to the root of the problems. The focus shifted from caring about people to making and or saving money.

The medical center was a Catholic Charities owned and operated hospital. It was here I first learned of a newer concept, "Clinical Pathways". Similar to to DRG's, Clinical Pathways were designed to describe the direction that a particular disease process should follow. For example, if you came to the hospital with Appendicitis and required surgery, you should be taking clear liquids post op, passing gas, taking semi solid foods and voiding (urinating) within 24 hours post op. Staples should be removed, steri-strips applied and you would be discharged with aftercare instructions shortly after these things occurred. If this did not happen someone was going to have to answer to someone.

This was all intended to streamline the cost of providing care. Stream lining care cost did not take into consideration we were caring for people not objects. People do not fit into neat little predictable boxes. One of the main factors not included in the calculations was that "Caring" takes time. It was not even a consideration that those providing the care were also people not objects. There was a time when people went into nursing because they "Cared" for people. They wanted to be able to show that "Care". This was made impossible by the implementation of systems like these. **The health care industry became a moneymaking business not a people business.**

In a typical shift on a Med Surg floor I might be assigned eight patients. By the end of that shift I probably took care of twelve or thirteen patients. Why? If a patient was discharged it opened a bed for some one new. If I had three or four discharges my total patient load was twelve. The hospital did not see it that way. At the end of the shift the census counted only eight. There was a column for admissions and discharges but the time factor was not a part of the census. In my earlier years patients were categorized by their care needs. Patients with heavy care needs (higher acuity) were grouped in assignments with patients with lesser acuity to help balance the load. This did help a little but we could not anticipate what type of patient we would get from shift to shift so this did not help were admissions and discharges were concerned.

Now I was an RN working in OB. The ratios were no longer two to one. Things were changing. Computers were the new things. We were now looking up and ordering lab work on the computer, checking orders over the last 24 hours and ordering meals. There was a time when the nurse did not have to do these things. We had help from a unit secretary also known as a ward clerk. Now we were responsible for our work and the work that others used to do for us. At times this even included housekeeping duties. The CNAs were of vital importance to us as well as our patients when it came to providing good care. Now we did not even have a CNA half the time. This was one of the reasons I left the hospital in Santa Barbara. There we had a patient load of six or seven. It was a little less than Med Surg because of the acuity level. We had an RN supervisor on the floor, a unit clerk, at least four licensed nurses and two CNAs to help with bedside care. Even with this kind of staffing we worked twelve hours almost non stop. We had a thirty-minute break if we were lucky and the company had already taken away our time and a half pay for any thing past eight hours. Before I left they reduced our staffing to one CNA for the whole unit. Each licensed nurse now had to do most of their own bedside care in addition to their other responsibilities. In short, the workload was increased. The time to do it in was not! The whole time the importance of maintaining the quality of care was emphasized. What a joke! I say that sarcastically of course.

If the truth were told to the public about being admitted to any hospital it would read something like this.

Dear Patient:

Upon Admission to our hospital we will do our best to provide you care but it is imperative that we do it with minimal cost to us. The high cost of technology combined with the increasing cost of living has made it impossible to make a profit so we have reduced our staff.

It may take a while for your light to get answered so hang in there and don't give up.

In an effort to save cost your linen will not be changed unless it is heavily soiled.

We only have one CNA assigned to your floor. The nurses are overloaded. You will be required to do as much for yourself as you possibly can.

You may only see your Doctor and nurse for a few minutes each day so have all your questions and concerns ready for them when they come to see you.

You or your insurance will be billed for the care you received from us not for the quality of your care or stay.

Be thankful you have healthcare available to you. We are not a hotel!

Sincerely,

The Management

All the while we the staff are being reminded that the patients are our customers. We would not have jobs if it weren't for our patients. (True). Answer your lights as soon as they go on! Do not have any overtime! If you do you may get in trouble. Don't make any errors such as medication errors! For a long time we the nurses simply clocked out first and then did our charting off the clock to avoid the pressure from management about overtime. Is that right or even fair? I've always been of the opinion that our patients need us! We in turn benefit from that need by getting paid! Therefore, both sides benefit from each other. Each position should be appreciated. We could have sick people without having anyone to care for them or hospitals to care for them in. We could be like other countries that don't make health care available to everyone. For some this is already the reality even in America. I'm a realist. I think it better to tell it like it is. Perhaps then we as a society won't take so many things for granted. If you are ever hospitalized I hope your trust is in God. Then if something goes wrong your trust is still in him to bring you through.

We hear horror stories about the mistakes that happen in hospitals and I do feel sympathy for the ones who have been the victims of certain horrors. I myself am uncomfortable with the thought of needing to be admitted to a hospital but that is because I know both sides. Most hospitals are not staffed well enough to provide good care. Good care takes time and time is money!

We as a society want the latest and the greatest technology but everything has a price tag on it. In exchange for good care we got advanced technology. Is that good or bad? Maybe it's both good and bad. For certain it is something we all have to accept. Should you expect good care when you are hospitalized? Absolutely! In addition to that you should realize what part you play in adding to the problem. Should we be compensated for gross negligence against us in a hospital setting? Yes. Should people sue for every little thing that goes wrong? I think not. After all man is not God even though some may think he is. There was a time when people understood that good and bad things happen to good and bad people. Now people think everything that happens is someone else's fault and they need to get compensated for everything. Each time a hospital is sued you may get paid but the Physician and the hospitals malpractice insurance is going to be effected. If it is affected too much guess what? The cost of providing services to the public is going to increase. If services cost too much, insurance companies don't make enough money so they increase the cost of insurance premiums to the consumer so in the end we all lose. I believe this is the reason behind the insurance reforms that came about with HMOs. They wanted to make more money.

Add the fact that society is more corrupt as a whole. We advocate promiscuity and fornication even abortion. I can't help but wonder what the financial impact to this country because of these life styles has been. The cost of treating STDs alone I'm sure have been staggering.

Let us not forget about the fraudulent activity that has occurred in the past such as Medicare fraud. In the long-term care arena this resulted in the implementation of the MDS (Minimum Data Set). This multiple page document, seven to eight, sometimes more pages long was implemented to provide better tracking to the Department of Health Services (DHS) of the care being provided to the elderly. Certain sections were directly related to the reimbursement a facility would receive for the care of that resident. In the long- term care environment nurses already had entirely too many residents to care for. When the MDS came along some facilities added it to the nurse's duties. Others hired MDS nurses to complete these records. For Medicare patients this document was to be completed within five days of admission, again at fourteen days, again at thirty, at forty- five and sixty days. All other admissions were done by fourteen days then quarterly then annually. The MDS was done manually then the information was entered into a computer and fed into the DHS databases. Routine charting was already sufficient to be classified as more then we could complete in eight hours if done well. Now some genius decided that more paper work would fix the fraud and abuse problems that

56

had become so prevalent to these facilities. It did make it easier for DHS to track status of the residents. To my knowledge DHS did not provide the computers to the facilities for this newly implemented program. They did not share the cost of or provide training to the staff that now had to learn to do MDSs. Nor did they pay the salaries for the new MDS nurses that some facilities had to hire to comply with the new regulations. Guess what? The cost of providing services went up! In some ways this did improve the quality of the care being offered. It also increased the stress and workload of the staff. Remember we still had the same amount of time to complete each added task and the same number of staff to do it with. Nursing was becoming a less desirable profession.

This is where burn out comes in to play. Nurses used to stay put for years. Some have managed to change with the times. To those who have managed to do this without compromising their integrity as a "Caring" individual I applaud you! Many simply pass the buck to the next shift nurse. After a while you feel hopeless and helpless. When you realize you cannot change the situation you try to harden your heart and do what you can do. Then you realize that is not who you are and you try again to do more. The cycle weighs on you emotionally and physically. You dread going to work. When I burned out beyond what a vacation or a few days off could do to refresh me, I looked for a change of environment.

One thing I never had a desire to do was work in management. I ended up in management. I was aware of the politics and power struggles that went along with being in management and I didn't want anything to do with it. To my surprise I received a call from a facility that I'd applied to work for while I was still going to school to become an RN. I initially refused an LVN position on the night shift at this facility because I would have been the only nurse at night taking care of seventy plus residents. I told them no thank you! They kept my application on file. Now the current DON needed an assistant. I was both excited and nervous about the opportunity. My burnout turned to hope that I could some how make a change in the business. I decided it was not good to be one of the ones who just complained about the way things were. It was better to try to be part of the solution to the problems. My manager said she was sad to see me go but we both knew this was a good opportunity for me. So I took the Job.

Chapter 9

The Villa was a seventy plus bed nursing home. The year was now 1997. They now had two nurses scheduled to work the night shift and three on days. Things appeared to be a little better. I was hired to be the Assistant Director of Nurses. Of course I was nervous but I felt good about this new level of responsibility.

Sheri was my boss. She was a great mentor. I learned so much about being flexible and new ways of retaining staff. I was much more rigid than Sheri. I did not understand how a professional person a licensed nurse could just not show up for an assigned shift. No call. No show. If I did that at any time in my career I knew I would no longer have a job. At Villa this was common. I could understand CNAs behaving like that more than I could professionals. During the difficult times in my life when I was having marital problems and my life was full of drama I still managed to call and let my employer know what was going on. I was learning rapidly how things were changing.

I studied every one and everything that went on around me. I took it all in. I called it using my assessment skills. When I worked on Med Surg, time was a precious commodity that we did not have much of so I learned to take in a lot of information in a very short time frame. In the midst of giving a med or checking on an IV site I also observed my patients color, expression, respiratory effort, noted if the patient appeared comfortable, etc etc. As a CNA I learned to look for these things while taking vital signs. These were important signs and symptoms. Over time I perfected these skills to the point that others noticed them. Shortly after I was hired at Villa my boss told me "the Administrator likes you, she says you are very observant". They agreed I could probably tell them everything that was going on in the facility. She was right. It didn't take long for me to see how extremely overworked the staff was including myself.

The med pass was terrible it took at least 3.5 hours just for the morning pass if done correctly. You see by this time DHS implemented very strict guidelines for doing everything. We had to wash hands between dispensing meds to each resident. That was basic. Now we had to wash our hands when giving eye drops to the same patient between each eye drop in addition to wearing gloves. We could not leave our cart unlocked to go into a room. In the early years we could leave it unlocked as long as it was facing the inside of the room, and it was in the doorway, reason being realistically a resident could not get into it that way. The cart was to remain in eye site even when we were in the room. Now it had to be locked no matter what. We could no longer crush medications that we did not have orders to crush. In times past residents were medicated against their will. The medications were disguised in applesauce to get them to take them. This was no longer permitted without consent from the responsible party and a doctor's order. Years ago you may have heard the horror stories of old people living in these homes being zonked and looking like zombies. Well a lot of that was done for staff convenience. It sounds cruel. Sometimes it was cruel but the other side of that was that nurses had thirty, forty, at one place I was responsible for fifty-nine patients at night with two CNAs. You may think that's no big deal because they are all sleeping. That was often not the case. All it took was one emergency like a fall or someone getting sick and you would get so far behind it was overwhelming.

DHS mandated that the meds be giving within a certain time frame. Most had to be given one hour before to one hour after the scheduled times i.e. 0900. Some had to be given with food, some without, like thirty minutes before a meal. This was difficult on a Med Surg floor with eight patients but quadruple difficult with thirty. That's only if you do it right. We were not supposed to give meds during a meal. We were not supposed to give things like eye drops in a public area. If the resident was in the hall we were supposed to take them to their room. Old people do everything much slower so everything takes twice as long to do for them but remember we still had eight hours to do three med passes, chart, do treatments on wounds, call doctors, deal with families, ancillary departments like Physical Therapy, Occupational Therapy, take off new orders, make rounds and supervise the CNAs. This did not include unexpected needs such as pain meds, falls and changes in conditions. I hope you get the picture. The State mandated these regulations with good cause but did not mandate sufficient staffing ratios. What's wrong with this picture?

Any way, I saw how bad things were for the staff. I would soon see how difficult things would be for me too.

I was very disappointed to see that the Assistant DON was basically expected to be the Jack-of-all-trades. Whatever the nurses could not get done, I did. When a nurse called off sick or did not show I had to work in their place. One time I actually worked a twenty- four-hour shift because there was no one to replace me. This was on top of my managerial duties.

In my early years of nursing we did not do IV therapy in nursing homes. Now we did. These areas were known as the Medicare Units or in some cases the Sub Acute Units. On our unit we had a few less patients but now our patients were not here to finish out their lives. They were here for rehabilitation. Some were very sick needing IV antibiotics, wound care, even Total Parenteral Nutrition. We were taking care of patients with central lines and feeding tubes. This required closer monitoring. The patients we cared for now were more like the patients we used to take care of in the hospital but in the hospital no one would expect you to have twenty or more patients. Now they did and the patient acuity was now much higher.

One day we had two emergencies at the same time in our Medicare Unit. One patient passed out in a wheelchair. I think the other coded! My nurse was already swamped.

I was very upset that day because while I was assessing one patient the other needed help too. The staff abandoned both patients and me. The CNA who was assigned to the group decided it was time for her to go to lunch even though I told her to stay with the first patient while I went to assess the next one. She was Philippine. I didn't know if she was that dumb, if she was playing dumb or if I was dealing with a language barrier. At that moment I did not care. All I cared about was that she abandoned her patients at a critical time. After I stabilized the patients and got them the help they needed, I sought out that CNA. I was furious with her but I was not allowed to show my feelings. Deal with the problem without making the person feel bad. Be considerate of their feelings. This was the new style of managing. Analyze the problem. Determine whether or not you did everything you could do to help this employee succeed in this situation.

This was neither productive nor was it effective in my opinion but I knew better than to ruffle too many feathers in my position so I followed the rules. I also knew that if I'd done something that stupid and inconsiderate as a CNA, LVN or RN there would be serious consequences to pay. I counseled the CNA in private. She insisted she was hungry and it was time for her to go to lunch. She didn't want to get in trouble for going to lunch late. I tried to explain to her that emergencies take priority over breaks and that she would be paid for her lunch if she had to miss it.

Under no circumstance are you to leave a critical patient unattended.

I was also disappointed that the rest of the staff did not stay to help us. I knew at that moment that something was drastically wrong in this place. We did not have adequate staffing! The nurse assigned to this unit was a very conscientious nurse. But even she was swamped. Actually she was swamped all the time. We had some good CNAs but we had too many CNAs that were head strong, insubordinate and uncaring. I began to feel afraid as I thought of what must go on in this building at night when there were even less staff around. This was not a one-time occurrence. Another time a code blue was announced over the intercom. The staff and I ran to the scene. As I got close to the scene my boss told me not to rush the patient was a "No Code" so I slowed my pace. When I got to the room the patient had expired. There was no more urgency true but I then noticed again how everyone else including the assigned CNA left the scene. While there was no more urgency there were still duties to be performed such as post mortem care. I did not fully trust some of my staff at that time so I assessed the patient for signs of life. There was no pulse, no respirations, and no vital signs. I prepared to do post mortem (after death) care but realized this was a game that certain people played. Pretend like you don't know how to do something then you won't have to do it. I decided I was not going to play that game. I called the CNA assigned to this patient and told her what needed to be done.

One day one of my RNs went to flush a central line. She reported that it was hard to flush. She thought it was plugged. I asked her did she report it to the MD. She casually replied no, I flushed it anyway. My heart started to race. I broke out in a sweat! It was against protocol to force flush a central line. In my experience it was standard nursing practice to apply color-coded tape to the plugged site. This warned others not to flush it. You notified the DR. and used the other ports instead. The danger was such that if you force flushed the line you could be forcing a blood clot into the person's blood stream. This action could cause a heart attack, CVA, Pulmonary Emboli or other complications. I was overwhelmed with the lack of knowledge and skill I saw on a day-to-day basis while supervising in this facility.

I have to tell you, this floored me. I wondered how it was that my training had been so strict. Why I had to be so precise when all around me was incompetence. I went into the office feeling shocked and confused. I explained to my boss what I'd just witnessed. She was not alarmed like I was. She simply stated, this is an area you have identified that we need to do some training in. I thought. That's it? What about what happens in the mean time before we put a class together? What if the ones who need the training don't show? I had questions and concerns. I felt some things were important enough that they should be dealt with right away. May be this was because I was green, new to management. Maybe it was because I was afraid. Maybe it was because I "cared" about the patient's safety and the legal implications of something like this but I let it go. I dealt with it the way I was told to. I informed the DSD of the need for staff training in this area and hoped for the best.

One day while making rounds I came upon one of our old school nurses doing a treatment. This resident had ulcers, wounds that were not healing. I watched in horror as she set up her supplies on the over bed table. The surface was not clean or protected. She did not wear gloves to protect herself or the resident from cross contamination. She did not set up her work area so that she could reach the things she needed. She kept using her dirty hand, the hand she'd already used to touch the wound, to pour the antiseptic and apply the clean bandages. I thought to my self, no wonder the patients wounds are infected/not healing. She keeps putting germs back in them. Back in the day we did treatments with out gloves. We changed diapers without gloves. We even started IVs without using gloves but that was back in the day. Standards had long since changed. In her defense I knew this nurse was antiquated and I know it is hard for some people to keep up with all the changes. But in my gut I was appalled. Again I told my boss about what I'd seen. She was not surprised. This was another area we needed to offer training in.

The morale was low. The reputation of this facility was poor. I know it takes time to bring about change but for me, in my life, most changes had to be made right away. I did not have the luxury of time. While I did not see the need to be ruthless concerning the changes needed, I did see the urgency and I felt, all that was needed was enforcement of a minimum standard. This was basic to me. I was beginning to see that basic to me was not basic to everyone else. After all these were basic Nursing 101 skills. This was not only basic skills level stuff I learned in school but also I'd practiced for the last fifteen years in some capacity or other.

While taking this all in I observed how the rest of the management team gathered for meetings each morning. This was around the time that stand up meetings were introduced to the nursing home environment. This new concept was introduced to facilitate better communication between department heads so that everyone could be on the same page. Each department involved with the care of the resident would know what was going on with them for example. The Dietician needed to know if someone was losing weight. Social Services needed to know too because the weight loss could be due to environmental changes. The resident could be depressed. I thought to myself, this is a good thing. But I soon saw that these meetings became a time to waist time in my opinion. What could be accomplished in fifteen to thirty minutes became an hour or so of socializing. I had rounds to make, supplies to check, MDSs to complete, resident and patient care needs to tend to, remember we were short staffed even when we were fully staffed. I did not understand wasting this valuable time. After the meeting then it was time to smoke and take a break. I did not smoke and rarely had time to take my breaks. This also frustrated me. Of course I knew better than to show how I felt so I endured the meetings until I asked my boss for permission not to. We agreed that she could pass on to me what ever I needed to know.

This is around the time that I began to learn about politics in the work place. I began to see that it was not enough to be dedicated, hard working; competent and pleasant you had to also "play the game". You are not here to accomplish the job. Not really because we are not here to accomplish the job. It was not the first time I'd encountered it but it was the first time I'd encountered it as a manager.

In the beginning I was invited to lunch with the other managers. I went a time or two. I listened as they talked about other peoples business, laughed and joked. I was not then and am still not a gossip so this did not interest me. In addition to that, the lunches away from the building would take up so much time that I decided I should not go any more. I told my boss of my frustrations. She voiced that she understood. However, I could see that I was alienating myself. Not intentionally but I felt, of necessity. I could not smooze and get my work done. Nor could I in good conscience avoid my duties in order to smooze. It did not feel right to me. I did appreciate the times when my boss said come on we are going to lunch! I know we have work to do but it will have to wait. We need a breather. I felt she was a hard worker too. She did not waste time. I felt we had a similar work ethic and neither of us abused those precious moments.

A few times, other managers were rude to me. They came to me in the hallways with their demands, talking down to me then walking away as if to dismiss me after they'd said their piece. I put up with this at first. What they did not know was that I was soft spoken, polite and very respectful but not a push over. I did not tolerate anyone being disrespectful to me because I spent so much time being respectful to others I felt I deserved the same thing in return. I was a team player but I was also an individual with feelings. These individuals were not responsible for my performance nor were they even in the nursing department so I politely but firmly let them know to never disrespect me that way again. If you have a request of me, just ask and I will comply if I am able. If not I will discuss it with my boss and see what can be done about your problem. If you cannot conduct yourself in this manner concerning me, don't ask me anything! Talk to my boss and she can direct me on your behalf.

In my home we were taught to say yes sir and yes maam. We were taught to respect each other. I could get in serious trouble if I was disrespectful to an adult or an elder even to my sister and brothers. I knew that all people were not raised this way but this was and still is my standard for dealing with others on any level. Treat them the way you want to be treated. The relationships changed for the better after these minor details were worked out. That is with everyone but Connie. I'll tell you about Connie a little later.

Things were not all bad. I met and worked with some very good nurses and staff. It was around this time that I met my new husband. He attended a Christmas party the job hosted with me. We had a wonderful time. My boss and co-workers gave me the thumbs up! They said he was good for me and they were right. Soon after this we became engaged.

My co-workers were so excited for me. During that time I needed surgery. I had Uterine Fibroids. They were so supportive. Several of them came to see me in the hospital. Sheri, my boss brought me one of my favorite things "French Vanilla" flavored coffee. Sheri always bought me special little gifts. She knew I liked Tweedy Bird so she often surprised me with Tweedy Bird gifts. I still have my Tweedy collection.

When the wedding day came, several of my co-workers and staff members attended. They brought beautiful gifts. This made that day even more special for me. To this day I get sentimental when I think about them. Marichu, Elsie, Nubia, Molly, and Joanne they are some of the names that come to mind.

Between the engagement and the wedding date, I quit. I tried to hang in there. Every day I went to work I prayed for strength to get through the day. The day came when I was no longer willing to endure. I kept my promise to my self and I took the advice of an instructor I met while working at Villa Maria. She told me to stay there for at least a year. It will look good on your resume. Then you can go anywhere in the business.

This day my boss was sick or out of the office for some reason. I had to go to stand-up in her place. She knew how I felt about stand-up so she told me to go but keep my mouth shut. Just listen! During the meeting the subject of completing the MDS's came up. This was one of my responsibilities so I had to give an answer for why they were not complete. In short the list of what needed to be completed had been changed that morning or possibly the night before at the end of the day. So I explained that we, the nurses were working on it.

The Social Services coordinator had a problem with my explanation. "We don't want to hear your excuses! She leaned her stocky body forward in her chair. Her face was stern; she glared at me through her glasses. Connie was supposed to be the mediator for resident problems. She was the one that residents were supposed to confide in if they had an emotional or social problem. The problem with that in my opinion was that Connie was mean. She was bossy and lacked any kind of empathy or people skills. I often cringed when I heard her address our patients in the hallways or their rooms. She teetered between being rude to being very intimidating. She did not intimidate me though. When she began to loud talk me in front of my peers about something that was not even her jurisdiction I firmly told her my explanation was not an excuse, it was a fact. She came back with more demands and insults. At this point my heart was beating fast. I was angry but was doing all I could to keep my cool. I told her she had no idea what the nurses, myself included dealt with on a day-to-day basis in this place. They would not understand because they sat in the office half the morning wasting time while the staff is out there busting there butts to get the job done! If you change the schedule at the last minute, common sense would tell you the change would create a problem with the time the MDS's are completed. To that statement the administrator, Lori became offended. She did not have a problem with Connie loud talking me in front of my peers even though she was not my boss. She was not even in my department. But she had a problem with me telling it like it was even though it was in my defense, because that statement reflected on her leadership skills. She told me I was out of line! I had no right to say what I was saying! I knew that if I stayed I would say more so I politely excused myself. I went back to my office. I was furious!

These are the same people who told me they stayed up late nights before survey and doctored charts so they would not get deficiencies. They called them survey prep parties. These are the same people that smoked half the day a way. If they worked half as much as the rest of us perhaps they could be more productive. The nerve! Long story short I resigned. I was at a place in my life that I no longer had the patients to put up with what I called foolishness. I knew I was a square and was not willing to force myself to fit into a circle.

From this experience I learned a lot about the long term care business. I also began to develop a reputation for being one who stood up for my nurses, something that was rarely being done but greatly desired by most nurses, my self included. We were becoming tired of all the impossible demands. We were responsible for the brunt of the care but received the least amount of support or respect for what we did.

Besides all of this I was for once in a long time excited about my future. I was engaged. I was planning my wedding. I had something beautiful to look forward to. I did something new. I resigned without having another job lined up. It didn't take too long before I landed another job. Another job offer came on top of the first one so life was looking good!

Chapter 10

The first new job was in Arroyo Grande. I applied for a night shift supervisor position. Instead they offered me a Position as Director of their Transitional Care Unit but shortly after I started working there another position I'd applied for came through.

Since becoming a DSD I had a desire to teach at the community college level. The local community college needed CNA Instructors. I was so excited and pleased about this new opportunity. I saw it as a chance to do something I really enjoyed and make a contribution to the medical field. We needed good CNAs. If the CNAs were good perhaps they would go on to become good nurses at some point in their careers. That was what we needed.

My excitement was short lived. Within the first few days of class I felt like quitting. There were two specific reasons for this. I will explain. First I learned the hard way that the reason the school needed new instructors was due to their lack of following the guidelines set forth by DHS to allow a college to offer CNA training. I learned from one of my students that the program had been shut down in the midst of a class the previous semester for noncompliance to the rules. This was later confirmed by several of my colleagues after I began to ask questions about what happened. I found out because this student became rather upset with me for enforcing the rules about the requirements for enrollment. This student was pregnant. She needed a written note from her Dr. stating she was able to lift a certain number of pounds safely. Her Dr. did not want to take the responsibility for making this statement so he just

all students had to have this clearance on record along with malpractice insurance due to possible liabilities. If they did not they could not attend class until they did.

The required hours of training were such that each student could only miss a very few days of class. When I explained this to the student she proceeded to tell me off in front of my class. She blamed me for all of her previous frustrations in dealing with the college because she was in the class that had been shut down. She accused me of acting like I owned the college. She behaved so badly I had to ask her to step outside. Like I said before being disrespected was something I did not tolerate well. I put her in check and told her she had to take it up with administration. Since I was following the guidelines as set forth naturally I expected the administration to back me up. Apparently they felt guilty or were intimidated by her loud rude behavior so instead of backing me they made an exception to the rule for her. She felt she'd won. I was not engaged in battle I was simply following the guidelines given to me. If you've ever been in a leadership situation like this you know you have to establish right away who's in charge or at least be able to hold your own when challenged. Now remember "respect" was a big part of my cultural upbringing. I lost respect for this student and the ones who made the decision to overlook her behavior. I was not prepared to defend my authority over and over again. I should have been told of the previous problems they'd had with the State. Instead they chose to hide it, even from the ones who would have to help smooth over the bad public relations. I was in no frame of mind to be disrespected by my students. I would have never even thought to behave so badly and talk to a teacher that way. I was now being exposed to the community in a whole new way. Students like this one acted as though I owed them something. I felt they thought I was working for them. As far as I was concerned I was working for the school. They had the privilege of getting an education. I had the experience and ability to give them an education and was glad to share my experience with them so it should have been a mutually gratifying experience.

When I went to school l was held to a very high standard at every level. I began to see that only a few of my students appreciated being held to a high standard. My standard was based on the curriculum, the same material I'd learned and practiced for years. It had not changed. I began to see that people had changed. What I endured during my training was now considered to be too much! "She acts like she owns the school." "She acts like this is her school." She has an attitude! These were the type of comments I received. My class was racially and culturally mixed but I only had one Black student in my class. She was excellent. That may have been because she was a mature person but I think the fact that she could relate to me made a big difference. Overall my students respected me. But there were some that would not follow instructions. This caused problems for me. Jim, my old administrator still ran the facility I was now teaching in. He came to me with complaints from the staff about my student's safety techniques when transferring residents. He had first hand knowledge of my abilities from when I'd worked there but he was concerned about his patients. This was a new breed. I pulled the students from the floor and reviewed transfer skills with them. They did not have to transfer residents in their last clinical site so I had them demonstrate their skills for me. Like my training, the clinical part of their training was done in a nursing home. They had to take care of real people. Believe you me there was always something to observe, research or do. If a student was bored in my class I felt it was because they were not trying to get everything out of the class there was to learn. Attitude is fifty percent of any job. I had students who were verbally aggressive, loud talking me in the clinical setting and the hallways but they complained I had an attitude problem when I corrected them. If one of my students was bored in the hospital setting I felt this was probably not the right career choice for them. During my training we never had time to be bored. I felt it was my job to cultivate them to be good CNAs not just CNAs. If you were going to pass in my class it would be because you earned it and you were competent. I felt my reputation was at stake. I wanted to be proud of my students and I wanted to hear good things about them when they left my class and went out to work in the real world. We lived in a small community.

In short my first experience with the college was horrible. I walked into a mess. I later learned that the term for a situation like this was "set up to fail".

When it came time for my first evaluation I was very nervous but I received a good evaluation. It included comments about my soft-spoken, gentle approach and positive rapport with my students and the facility staff. Out of the ten categories observed I scored the highest in six, the second highest in four and had no substandard areas. But the school had a policy that they asked the students to evaluate the instructors too. My students were divided in their evaluation of my teaching skills as an instructor. The class seemed to be split fifty fifty. The way things started with this class I thought fifty fifty was good. I knew there were students who didn't like me and students whom I didn't enjoy teaching. But the deans were very concerned about the students' comments. They wanted to know what "I" was going to do about this. I gave a written explanation of the events that occurred in my class and the challenges I faced. They did not take responsibility for any of it but accepted my plan of action for improving my teaching skills. They also encouraged me not to try to make the students become "competent" but told me to simply introduce them to each skill. Keep the expectations low! Do not push them too much. They are not LVN or RN students. I found this to be very interesting. Pushing them to succeed in the basic CNA skills like following instructions was now considered to be too much. I wasn't teaching anything that was remotely equal to LVN or RN status. It was too much coming from a Black person! Just being Black seemed to generate a certain animosity from certain students who didn't like instruction from me or me observing them. It was perfectly normal for me to be instructed and observed as a student but "too much" for me to expect others to expect it.

I say this because for years the college employed White nurses as instructors. To my knowledge they never had a Black one, not before me nor after me. Rose was one of the old timers. Rose was tough but fair. She knew her stuff. She held her students and staff to a high standard. She was well known for teaching at the college and working at the local hospital. I had great respect for Rose. When I explained my perception of how I interacted with my students to Deborah, one of the of the Deans she found it to be interesting because she said Rose was the same way you are but the students never complained about her. I wanted to tell her that is because I am young and I am Black! Other cultures do not take kindly to receiving instructions from Blacks, competent or not. They may accept it better if you are an older person but they don't like it. Instead, I played the game. I decided I would not push any of the students unless they displayed a desire to learn more. Again it was clear I had to go above and beyond the call of duty to keep the same job and get the same respect that others got automatically. The Deans' own evaluation didn't seem to hold any weight after certain students complained.

The fact that I stuck with it should have given me a great sense of satisfaction but it didn't. After all I worked hard for everything I got in my career. Very few, took me under their wing and nurtured my skills or me. If I didn't get it right I was reprimanded or at minimum had to do it over until I got it right. I stayed with the college a little over a year. My next class went well. Out of twelve students only one had negative comments about me this time. I could have viewed this as an improvement in my performance. But I knew that I was no longer giving my all but rather trying not to make waves. I was not accepted for who I was but was forced to conform to others expectations of me. I spent too much of my life doing that already and I was not about to start that whole process over again. In my school experiences my instructors didn't have to prove them selves to me. I had to prove myself to them. So I quit!

It was at this time that I remembered the Black instructor I had when I was in LVN school. Now I could relate to how she may have felt being a minority in the health care profession.

Fortunately for me the college was not my only employer. I was only working part time for them and part time in Montecito at a place I called the Mexican Mafia Head Quarters.

Chapter 11

The Mexican Mafia headquarters was a beautiful facility nestled in Montecito California. Montecito was an exclusively rich White community about one hour and fifteen minutes away from Lompoc. The grounds were beautiful. The facility was state of the art. Money was of no concern. It was a retirement community. The residents bought into the community for life. They had independent living facilities, assisted living facilities and long term care facilities. This set up provided care to its residents at any level they could possible need. I'd never heard of a place like this. I thought I hit the jackpot. I felt so blessed.

Carol interviewed me first. She was the Director of Education. Actually she was the DSD. That is what she would have been called anywhere else. Here she was the Director of Education. Then Diane interviewed me. She was the Administrator. Initially she was concerned because I'd quit several jobs prior to applying with them but after talking with me she decided to give me a chance. She however warned me that there were bigots in the community and felt I should be aware of this fact. Again I was one of two Black people working in the whole facility, more specifically the whole campus. The other person worked in Security. He was a very nice guy who'd been there for a long time. I actually did not know for a long time that he was Black. His complexion was so fare that I thought he was Hispanic.

This place was huge. It was an old Victorian style historic site. It had its own auditorium and its own clinic. The big house was where the historic family lived in their day. Now it is where the administrative offices were placed. The house contained a ballroom, a huge tea parlor and library. These were just some of its' beautiful features. In the rear was a beautiful lawn where the social events took place each year. I could imagine how grand the festivities must have been in its day. It truly reminded me of the many stories I'd read as a youngster in high school about the Victorian era. Surrounding the lawn was the servant's quarters. One of the highlights for the resident's was Lawn Bowling. They did this on a beautifully manicured lawn. The dining facility looked more like a restaurant. They had waiters and waitresses. They had ground keepers and on-site security to mention a few of the perks.

I expected to have some problems just because I was Black. I was familiar with these ratios but I had not gotten tired of them yet. I knew that dealing with this age group I was bound to face some prejudices. It was part of the territory but I knew I could do the job and I wanted to work in a nice place such as this. They matched the pay I was getting at the college. So I accepted the position.

Let me back track. I got married, started working part time for the college and then started working part time at the Mexican Mafia headquarters all in the same month. The year was 1998.

Things were fine on the surface. I shared a big office with by boss Carol. She was White of course. Carol was nice. She was knowledgeable. She'd been there a long time. She seemed to enjoy teaching and was well liked by her co-workers and the CNAs. I was hired as the Assistant Nurse Educator. So my job was primarily to assist her. I did not have my own desk because we were planning to move our office soon. So I worked around Carol as best I could. Carol was good at lots of things but needed help. I did things like filing and maintaining records. I had very little to no interaction with the staff or the residents. I was being used more as a secretary. I was happy to work at such a beautiful place so I just did what was asked of me.

Not long after I started, Diane called me into her office. She told me she was very impressed with me. "You are the only Black person on this campus yet you walk around with your head held high". She was impressed with my confidence. I wasn't sure if this was a compliment or not but thanked her for sharing her observations with me.

Things were pretty uneventful. Other than some remodeling and relocating, not
looking forward to getting a desk and having a space to work from. For some reason we did not stay there long. Finally we relocated to a class room in the underground parking area. It was actually a good place for holding classes. We had lots of cabinets

and closet space for storage. We had the latest video equipment, computers and resources available to us. I thought surely I would get a desk now. I just wanted a place to work from to call my own. I prided myself in being organized but found it difficult to do without having my own space. Carol eventually provided me with a very small utility cabinet to work from.

As far as I knew no one had a problem with me being there. The only complaint I'd had against me came from one of the residents. This person told Diane they saw me walking across the campus one day eating a piece of fruit. This was not acceptable and it offended them. I asked Diane if there was a policy directing staff not to eat outside or only eat in designated areas outside that I was not aware of. Of course there wasn't. To this person I was the hired help. I wondered if they knew I was working in management. But I knew that it probably did not matter to them. I was offended but I took it in stride. I did not eat outside any more.

After probably a year or so I began to get bored. I began to feel frustrated. I began to pray about my feelings. "Lord, this is the best job I've ever had. This place is absolutely beautiful. Why do I feel frustrated? What is wrong with me? His reply to me, "because you are out of place". After some soul searching and examination I realized what the Lord was saying to me. I was a qualified teacher. I'd grown thru the ranks. Once you grow up so to speak, you cannot be content with the same old thing. You become stagnate.

You see, six months after I got this position I had a profound spiritual experience. Although I was raised in the church and had been a Christian most of my life, there were times that I'd strayed from my faith. Now I had a new commitment to the Lord Jesus Christ and was having an experience with him like I'd never known before. Now he was not distant to me. He was very real and I talked to him about everything, the good the bad and the ugly things in my life. When I had questions I asked. I prayed about my daily life. So I prayed about this too.

There was a time in my life I never wanted to be in management. I didn't want to deal with the politics or play the games people played in management. But I'd grown to the place were I now wanted to solve problems not just deal with them. I wanted to make a difference. I wasn't teaching. I wasn't solving problems or contributing in any real way. I felt it would have been more cost effective for Carol to have an office secretary for an assistant then me because I was not functioning as an RN. Although money was no problem for this facility I felt like I was getting something for nothing and this bothered me. I know a lot of people prefer this but it bothered me.

I still did not have my own desk. Whenever I asked Carol about this she said she was waiting to see if I was going to work out before she bought me a desk. I was not interacting with the staff or residents much. I felt as though I was being hidden on purpose and was not being used for my qualifications. I needed stimulation. I wanted to feel like I was part of the team.

A few times I covered for Carol on the floor. That was when I began to see what the facility was really like. I began to experience the facility culture. The facility had been without a DON for almost a year. This puzzled me. In a beautiful place like this with all of the resources, good staffing ratios and the good pay, why would they have trouble retaining CNAs and a DON?

All of the Administrative staff were White. The majority of the CNAs were Hispanic. The residents were White and rich. Here they did not abide by the same rules as other long-term care facilities did. And DHS did not require them to. This place was more like a hotel. At least half of the residents had personal care attendants that came and went as they pleased. There was no accountability for them. The CNAs also came and went as they pleased. They took long lunches without clocking out and without letting their nurses know they were leaving. They hung out in the charting room as long as they wanted talking on the phone and socializing. They left the residents unattended during meetings. All of the CNAs would leave the floor. They repeatedly left them in the DR eating unattended. They ate from the resident's trays while feeding them and socializing with each other. They did not attend In-services (required training) when scheduled. They did not brush the residents' teeth on a regular basis. They did not put them down for naps. They did not turn them frequently when they were in bed. They refused to use the hydraulic lifts for safe transferring of the residents. They would not take them to activities. The activity director had to go get the resident's herself. No wonder so many of the resident's had personal attendants. All of theses things were against DHS regulations and the facility policies and procedures. The Mexican CNAs were running this place!

For a long time I'd wondered why there was such poor participation in In-services when they were scheduled. Carol didn't seem to mind. Carol was teaching a class, several of our current students were repeating the class because they did not bother to keep their certifications current and had worked some time in the center before this was discovered. Carol finally shared some of the past history of the facility with me and its problems.

The staff had already caused quite a few of the nurses to leave and they got rid of

Diane the administrator. She was trying to bring the facility into compliance and they were not having that. They complained about her and signed a petition to get rid of her. It worked.

Carol decided some time ago if you can't beat them; join them so she did not try to bring about any changes. Now I realized why every one liked her, she didn't make any waves.

I was not in the position to bring about change so mostly I observed the happenings.

After a while they hired Sally to be the new DON. Sally seemed nice. She dressed well. I believe she was in her sixties. She drove a beautiful gray Mercedes Benz. I later learned the facility leased it along with her upscale living quarters. Talk about fringe benefits!

I thought maybe now there would be some needed direction and oversight. I thought perhaps the problems I'd seen were simply due to lack of leadership. Sally began to make some changes for the better. We started having staff meetings. She fought to improve the wages and won the fight against her opposition. I did not think we needed to improve the wages because they were already good but I did see the value in increasing the wages on the weekends because that was when we were really coming up short staffed.

It seemed as though Sally wanted to show the staff she cared about their needs. I understood this approach. It was Sally who hired the only Black CNA I'd seen working there. The day I saw her I was so excited. She also seemed both excited and relieved to see me. I introduced myself and asked how she was doing. To that she replied not so well. She thought this was going to be a great place to work but it was not what she thought it would be. She told me certain members of the staff were giving her a hard time. She did not disclose to me who they were. I encouraged her to hang in there. I think she told me she came from the LA area. She was articulate and well groomed. I don't think she lasted a week. I was about to see why.

By this time I'd been here for two years. I had several evaluations', each one favorable with no sub standard areas and raises accompanied them. I still did not have a desk. I began to do more and have more interaction with the staff. I was invited to attend DSD meetings, administrative meetings and lunch with Carol and Denise. I even won an award for being a valuable and loyal employee. At the DSD meetings I was tolerated. It was apparent to me that most of the participants did not see me as belonging in their midst. Remember I was the only Black person. In the administrative meetings I was tolerated. The people were polite but not interactive with me. I thought they actually invited me to participate in some way so when they asked me how I was doing with the CNA's I told them. It was immediately clear they were stunned to here my views.

When I went to lunch with Carol and her friend Denise I was disgusted. They frequently talked about people they didn't like, sometimes to the point of sounding cruel. This was not for me. So again I separated myself from this type of behavior. In addition to that they would take one, sometimes one and a half hours for lunch when we were only allowed thirty minutes. At first I convinced myself this was ok because I was with my boss but after a few times I began to feel guilty. I felt like I was committing fraud.

Somewhere between my second and third year of employment I was finally given more responsibilities. The facility was making some changes and they needed Carol to increase her responsibilities throughout the campus. She asked me to teach the next CNA class. I was glad to. This was a way I could contribute.

Like so many other facilities we were having trouble retaining staff (hum). The facility already had the approval to offer classes. We just needed to reestablish and start the classes again.

This project supplied me with the stimulation I needed so I got busy ordering supplies. There was no evidence that there was ever a program in place, only some old sign off sheets that were incomplete. We needed books, uniforms, name badges and supplies for lab time. There was lot's to do and I enjoyed doing it. I created quizzes, test and the class syllabus. We advertised, we interviewed and before we knew it it was time to start my first class.

Just like when I was teaching in Lompoc, I enjoyed this class. I was engrossed in every aspect of it, lecturing, demonstrating, explaining and re-explaining. By the end of the day I was drained because I gave so much of myself. But I enjoyed my work.

Soon we began to have problems. I should have expected it. I was teaching my

performing according to the regs so this created a conflict. My students returned to class with lots of questions and complaints each time they worked on the floor. Knowing this could cause them to be targeted for ill treatment I tried to teach them to do what they'd been taught without ruffling any feathers. Do not correct the CNAs but do follow your own conscience. You are the one who wants to be able to sleep at night. You will have to go before the state board to pass your exams and you do not need to pick up bad habits. This did not work. The staff became hostile towards them and me to the point where I told Carol I needed her help as head of the department to intervene. She sympathized with me but was not willing to do anything to help the situation. We pressed on and completed the program. Nine out of ten students passed without any difficulty. One student had to retake a portion of the test. I did not know until then that this had never happened before.

From what I was hearing, only three or four students completed and past the classes before. I was both proud and frustrated to hear this news. I put so much of myself into teaching my students. I did everything I could to help them succeed. It was such a joy for me to see when the "light" of a students understanding came on and know they got it! But I also knew that if I'd had a failure rate of six out of ten at any time as an instructor teaching any class I would not keep my job for long.

The double standard was apparent to me again. It was also becoming apparent that I'd created a few enemies now due to my success with this first class. It only takes a few bad apples to create havoc. When I monitored my students, the staff would complain, "Carol never did that". When I complimented any of my students I was accused of having favorites.

On the flip side the nurses were beginning to trust me. I was developing stronger relationships with other staff members so all was not bad. They were beginning to ask me questions and share their concerns with me. Trust is a very important part of any relationship. It seemed that trust was developing.

January 16, 2001, I was at work. I was in the stairwell. I'd been taking the stairs as much as possible in an attempt to get in shape. I was now in my thirties and gaining weight was easy to do. I ran into Sally on the stairs. She asked me if I was interested in a new position. She wanted to know if I would consider becoming a supervisor over the CNAs. She went on to tell me she liked my style, my way of doing things. She felt I had the background and the experience to do the job. The CNAs would not be able to manipulate me. She warned they would be resentful of my presence a fact that I was already aware of. They would not like my being there because they were not used to being supervised. Sally made it clear she was getting up in age and did not have the stamina needed to bring about the necessary changes but assured me she would back me up. They would have to get in line or be let go. As incentive she offered me a raise from 23.00 to 25.00 per hour. I told her I would give it some thought and let her know.

The interesting thing about this whole conversation was that a week before, I'd had a dream that foretold it would take place. If you recall I told you I am a dreamer. I started having significant dreams when I was in RN school. Now I had them on a regular basis.

From my dream journal dated 1/ 8/ 01, I wrote:

Talking to old boss about wages

? 25.00 an hour

(Cathy Wat......) She's informing me

With this kind of money you should be running this department.

Don't tell anyone though, others watching, they don't need to know, it could cause problems

Scenery switched

Going through big hotel

Trying to move people from room to room safely

Saw huge pretty patio, trees, pool scene then went to Dorina

Side note from the Lord

I will be taking you off your job (in about a week)

My interpretation at the time of the dream

Cathy = feelings of distrust/incompetent.

She was someone in my past that I did not think highly of

Dorina= painful experiences

Mistreatment, used me, jealousy, inferiority complex

Conclusion

Painful past coming to repeat it self

Although I had frequent dreams I did not always understand them. I sensed it was a caution of some kind but felt I should accept the position anyway. So I did. It would increase my hours. I would continue working part-time for Carol and pick up a few days a week as supervisor for Sally. From the onset I faced severe attacks from the pack. That's why I named them the Mexican Mafia.

Sally and I decided I needed to be visibly present in the facility because for a long time there had been no oversight. The day I moved into my office, correction as I was moving into my office, members of the Mexican Mafia gathered together at the nurse's station across the hall and began to openly complain about me because my office was now what used to be their charting area/social area. They marched into my office and boldly aggressively let me know they did not want me there. "Why are you here?" "You are here to watch us aren't you? We don't want you here!" Talk about intimidating! My heart was pounding but I held my own. Choosing not to be aggressive in return I instead explained that my role was to help bring about some changes. No one was saying they weren't doing a good job but we just wanted our facility to be the best it could be. Sally requested my help and I would be an advocate for them as well, if they have any concerns. They didn't buy it. This was their turf and they were not going to give it up without a fight!

Instead of going in as a dictator I opted to hold meetings with the staff. I introduced myself and explained what my new role would be. I thought this approach would be less threatening. After several meetings I began to implement some basic guidelines like reviewing the proper chain of command, job descriptions and guidelines for breaks. The sad thing to me was that these things were basic nursing 101 issues. How had things gotten this bad?

The Mafia was rude, defiant and insubordinate, openly and blatantly they attempted to sabotage my efforts. In spite of the flack I received I began to see progress. Now the nurses were confiding in me, telling horrible stories of how the Mafia had threatened other nurses in the past with physical bodily harm if they did not succumb to their demands. That was why, they said, other nurse's left. They were afraid of them! When they had problems I encouraged them to document their concerns I would take them to Sally. They would be addressed. Repeatedly I was told "we have reported our concerns to Sally she does not do any thing about them". They reported not only does she not respond, she hides in her office when the going gets tough. Now I had a real problem. If Sally did not back them she may not back me. One nurse actually got down on her knees and thanked me for being there. She said for the first time in several years she was glad to see the CNAs actually working when they arrived to work the PM shift. Usually they wasted two hours socializing before they did anything. By then it was time for dinner.

From day one, I kept Sally informed of my every move. I discussed my plans and sought her input for all major decisions. She was supporting me to my face but doing the opposite behind my back.

I didn't know that Sally was undermining Carol too. I believe that was how Carol saw it. Carol was not happy that I was working for Sally. Although I liked Carol I was glad to now have more responsibility, a desk and my own office. I guess the real problem was that I was effective. At one time Sally even told me I was doing a good job. The staff was working better. They were attending training classes more and the residents were reporting that they were getting better care. Sally did not like that! She began to side with the CNAs. When I confronted her about her betrayal she promised she'd be more supportive. She lied!

In addition to supervisory duties I was given the responsibility of conducting the CNA In-services. Whenever a member of the Mafia was present in my class things were tense. The defiance and rude behavior continued to the point that I resorted to more aggressive methods of dealing with them. Following all the proper procedures I gave some written warnings and terminated one of them. Sally did not back me up instead she overturned my warnings and the terminations classifying them as "misunderstandings". When I gave a favorable evaluation to one of my former students she redid it because the Mafia heard about it and didn't approve of it. In short she set me up to fail.

During the next four months things went from bad to worse. It was clear now that I was on my own. Carol distanced her self from me. Sally had nothing to offer me but to tell me of the complaints that the Mafia brought against me. When I asked for specifics "what am I doing wrong"? She replied, "It's nothing they can put their finger on". One of the staff that liked me and had been there for a long time told me, "You are dealing with a cultural issue". "They, Hispanics don't like Blacks telling them what to do". She was Hispanic too. I sought advice. I went to the Social Services person. She was Hispanic. I suggested cultural awareness classes to try to improve the working relations. She did not see the need for this. I went to Human Resources and finally I wrote a letter to the Executive Director. In the midst of all this Sally hired another RN to be a Nursing Supervisor. Her name was Susan. Susan was White. At first I liked Susan. She was a new RN with two years of experience. She had no other experience in nursing. Susan had an abrupt way about her. She was to the point. Several staff members reported to me she made them cry because of her direct approach. In spite of this I thought she was exactly what we needed. I thought we would be a good team. But I soon noticed that the Mafia responded to her favorably! Sally even praised her approach and suggested I "follow her example." How? Become White! That was the final straw. The stress began to take its toll on me. No one supported me. At Sally's suggestion I relinquished handling problems when they arose. "Let her be the bad guy for a while". The insubordination continued anyway.

For the first time in my career I was sure my race was an issue. I couldn't change that. I didn't want to change that. I was not and have never been ashamed of being Black. There have been times I have been embarrassed by some of the behavior my people have involved them selves in. I have grieved to see the standards of my people lowered after the tremendous price our ancestors paid for the freedoms that we now have in an effort to assimilate. I made up in my mind a long time ago that I would not compromise my standards to fit in or keep any job and wasn't about to start now.

I waited for a response from the Executive Director. I'd written a complete report on what was going on, explaining the quality of care issues, as well as the aggressive behavior towards me. It took a lot of courage and several days for me to complete my complaint. I was disappointed when I read his reply. Dear Diane, "I am surprised and disappointed by your comments." "I will give this matter my careful attention over the next several weeks". I never heard from him again. He did not even call me in for a meeting!

As if things weren't bad enough I added fire to the flames when I acted as an advocate on behalf of one of our residents. This resident had an open wound that we were treating. It was deep, cutting through her fatty tissue exposing the muscles and flesh below. Sally set up a demonstration in an effort to show the nurses how to care for this wound. As she proceeded to demonstrate I observed with tears in my eyes as the resident cried out in pain. The wound bled and the resident cried out louder. Sally poked and prodded until she was done with the treatment. The resident apologized for her tears not wanting to be a problem.

Acting independently, I reviewed the steps of the procedure afterwards to see if the resident had received pain medication prior to the procedure being done. She had not. Upon learning this I was furious! I felt she was in severe pain at the time because her cries were so severe. They pierced my heart so much that I heard her cries in my sleep that night after the procedure. Now I knew why. It is standard procedure to medicate patient/resident prior to giving care that is likely to cause discomfort. Examples of this include wound care and physical therapy.

To ensure that this did not happen again I discussed the pain medication needs of the resident with the nurse on duty and made arrangements to have them given routinely as well as prior to wound care. I also instructed the nurse to evaluate the effectiveness of the medication itself and notify the MD if it was not effective. I then established a place to store all of the needed supplies and began to observe the nurses when they did the wound care procedure. One of the nurses had a problem with my intervention and instructions. She told me Sally says to do it different. By this point Sally was on my last nerve and I did not want to hear anything Sally had to say about anything so my reply to the nurse's statement was "I don't care who says what! We must use aseptic-clean techniques when doing this procedure". In addition to being concerned about the patients comfort level I was also concerned about introducing contaminates into the wound because the nurse's were not even preparing a clean surface to work from when doing this patients treatment. My job is to educate, that is what I am doing, educating you!

I believe the nurse reported my comments to Sally. I really did not care! I had no respect for Sally. She had no backbone. But most of all she had no integrity! She had set me up and made me the bad guy to make her self look good.

I began to look for my own solution. Some people say if you can't beat them join them. Well I was not capable of doing that so I began to look for another job.

By some chance meeting my husband heard about a new opportunity that would be opening up. A brand new facility was under construction in Lompoc. They would be needing a DON. He was very excited about this opportunity. He was confident I had a good chance of getting the position. I have to say I was not that confident. I was loosing my confidence. I had been abused in a manner that violated my very personality. What was it about me that caused these people to treat me so bad? I searched myself. I'd tried over and over to adapt. I tried different approaches. I cried. I prayed. Lord if there is any thing about me I need to change, I am willing to change. Just show me what to do. I could not win. How could people be so cruel? I wasn't looking for more stress at this point in my life. These were some of the very reasons I did not want to be a manager in the first place. My husband continued to encourage me. He said, "Diane you have been in nursing for almost twenty years. You have done a lot of things. All you have to do is draw from your experience and you will be alright". I began to remember other DONs I'd worked for. I remembered the stories that my LVN instructor told us about her career. Several of these nurses were very young, in there twenties when they were given DON positions. I was now thirty-eight years old, nearly forty and this was the first opportunity that came my way to be a DON. This to me was another example of the double standard that I was graded by, not only myself but also many other Blacks I'd heard about. I just hadn't experienced it for myself until now. I'd gone through so much to get this far that it did not seem fare that others had opportunities placed in their laps right out of nursing school.

I decided to apply for the position. I thought about all the good things we could do. I say we because I knew that nursing is a team concept. I would not be successful without a close knit qualified team. This could be the chance of a lifetime, an opportunity to create the type of environment that I and other nurses longed for. I wanted our facility to be the kind of place that most places were not. There would be no big I's or little U's. We would be a team. I received a call asking if I'd come for an interview. I was extremely nervous. We met at a local restaurant. There were two of them. I began to relax as we laughed and talked. It did not feel like an interview. Several days later I got another call. Now they wanted to meet with me at the facility site. This time there were three of them, the Owner, His side kick, and an Administrative Consultant. They asked questions. I asked questions. It went well. They offered me the position. I was blown away! What a blessing. What a blessing! I couldn't believe it. I was going to be a DON. The thought of this both excited me and frightened me. The facility was not open yet. It was still under construction so I would only be part time until the construction was complete then I would become full time.

I was more than glad to turn in my notice when I returned to work. I wanted to quit on the spot. Instead I met with the HR person. I requested a copy of my employee file for the road. I asked Dorrie, she was the HR director, if she'd received any feedback about my concerns. She had not. I knew I had a good record. I wanted my file as proof of that because I suspected they might try to add something derogatory to it so they could fire me. I asked Dorrie point blank. "Are they going to fire me?" She denied that they were. I went on to tell her I heard a rumor they were looking for a way to get rid of me. She again denied these allegations stating she had not heard this rumor. Then I turned in a notice to both Sally and Carol explaining that I have a new opportunity available to me and I planned to take it. It is only part time right now so I will continue my part time position as Assistant Educator not as a Supervisor, until it works into full time. In spite of how bad things were I did not want to leave them hanging. This was not all I wrote. I included my thanks and appreciation for the opportunity to work at such a beautiful facility. I'd learned so much both positive and negative things about the business. Things I knew would enhance my career and that I'd keep them posted as things changed etc. etc. I'm giving the short version right now. I did not get a response from anyone.

Several days later Sally called me to her office. When I arrived at her office I was surprised to see Carol there too. I got a sick feeling in my stomach! Sally spoke for them. We got your notice and have decided it would be best for all concerned if you move on! She handed me a check. I was stunned! You're firing me I asked? Oh no! She replied. You have a good record with us you're a good employee. We just think it would be better if you move on since you have a better opportunity any way, besides that we don't think we need another supervisor and we won't be teaching any more CNA classes. If you are not firing me than why didn't you respond to my notice by discussing this with me? I've been here almost three years! I have a good record! There is nothing bad in my file! I turned to Carol. I'd known her the longest. Why didn't you just tell me what you were thinking? I didn't know! She replied. In that case, I'd like to make it clear. I do not appreciate being handled in this manner. I knew they were lying! I knew they were conniving and plotting to get rid of me and that this was the only legal way they could come up with to do it. It was not enough that I would be moving on. They had to have the last say in the matter. The underlying message was how dare you leave us! We tell you when to leave! So leave! I went on to tell her I felt I was and am being treated this way because of the differences in culture, translation I'm Black! The staff had even told me so! To my comment Sally said, "I think any one who took this position would have been treated the same way. Your problem is, you need to learn to pick your battles more wisely. You need to learn the politics of the business! To that I replied. I've never been a politician!

I say what I mean and I mean what I say. I have no hidden agendas. To me she was saying. Ha Ha. I got you! I experienced again what it was like to be "set up to fail". Believe you me it did not feel good. Perhaps Sally was sincere in the beginning when she'd approached me for help. It was now apparent that she could not do the job but also did not want anyone else to do it either.

I was in a daze. I went to my office to gather my things. I called my husband to tell him the bad news. I'd been fired! He met me at the job and followed me home to make sure I was ok. The ride home was a blur. I was on automatic. When I made it home and stepped out of my car my husband was there for me. Thank God he was! Suddenly my knees were weak. Everything turned hazy. He helped me get inside the house and sat me in a chair. I began to cry! Before I knew it I was hyperventilating. My kids came to see what was wrong. My husband placed a bag over my face and reassured them I was all right. After a time, I calmed down.

Over the next several days I replayed all the events during my employment over and over in my head. I searched myself. I prayed. Although I had a new job lined up already this experience really disturbed me. If they didn't need another supervisor why didn't they just allow me to go back to doing DSD work until my new job became full time? If Carol didn't need help with DSD work, why was another nurse now assisting Carol with DSD needs? Why didn't Sally have a problem with Susan's' approach to the staff? I had so many questions. I tried to resolve them in my mind but could not.

I suddenly remembered the dream I'd had shortly before Sally offered me the position. Now it made sense. The Lord was showing me not to trust her. He was showing me the pain and agony that awaited me if I accepted her offer. Then I remembered another dream I had a few weeks before this day. This was a day when I was feeling the stress of work so much that I took the day off. While taking a short nap I dreamed this:

I was at a table/desk in an office

Somehow I noticed that some time had gone by and I hadn't got my work done...........

Realized I couldn't move, I was slumped/leaning in my chair,

I couldn't talk

After a while I started trying to mutter words to ask for help. No one could hear me. I kept trying. Somebody help me! I repeated.

Then I could see people. They helped me out of my chair and placed something on my face, I thought it was Oxygen (O2)

I tried to fight with it at first

People all around

Waiting for help

I asked the Lord, am I going to die now?

He said no, not for a long time

This was what just happened to me. The desk/table office represented my job. There was work I was trying to complete. I was numb all the way home. When I hyperventilated my husband placed a bag over my face, I needed Oxygen. I felt like I was going to die. I panicked. The Lord showed me how things were going to turn out.

At first I could not understand why I felt compelled to take the position if this was to be the out come. I wanted to sue them for wrongful termination. I found a lawyer who was representing another ex employee of this same facility who did not fit in because he was a good nurse. The lawyer confirmed I'd been wrongfully fired, said my case would possibly strengthen the other employees case. He told me to wait to hear back from him concerning how we'd proceed from here. Periodically I checked with him for updates. Then, mysteriously about a week before my statute of limitations time-line came I got a letter from him telling me he could not represent me at this time. It had taken me more than a week to find him so I knew I wouldn't find a new lawyer in time enough to meet my deadline. I came to realize and accept that a real Leader is made through adversity. Leadership skills are not acquired with a diploma. They are not gained because someone gives you a job. A true leader is going to pay a price. Have you heard the term "Pay the cost to be the boss"? Well, I was paying the cost! Every leader is going to be disliked, sometimes hated. The Bible says, Woe when all men speak well of you! If every one likes you something is drastically wrong with you (reference to being a Christian). I concluded that if I had the chance to do it over again I'd do it the same way. That meant I gave it my all. I did my best, so I licked my wounds and moved on. For good measure I did write a letter to the Board, in which I shared my concerns and my attempts to resolve them. They said they would direct the Executive Director to investigate the pertinent facts of the circumstances I'd reported. I knew what that meant so I took the experience I'd gained and prepared for my next venture.

Chapter 12

The Gardens was the highlight of my nursing career. It was a beautiful building designed to attract the attention of any one who was looking for shelter from the rain. The name implied it would be a safe haven. That is what I envisioned when I heard the name.

The central coast is known for its Missions. All along the coast you will see Mission Bells. They are representations of the benevolent work that used to go on in this region.

When I was first hired at the Gardens, it had no name. It was a beautiful building still under construction located in Lompoc California. This was great for me because it was ten minutes from my home.

Understandably I was nervous about the uncertainties related to this project. The walls were not up. The framework was visible. I'd never been involved with a project of this magnitude. There was already bad publicity associated with the building. A major provider of health care services previously owned it. This company owned several long term care facilities but had some legal troubles related to some major law suits that came against the facilities they owned in Santa Barbara. These troubles resulted in their inability to complete the construction of this building. It now had a new owner and construction was under way.

There was great concern in the community about the coming of this new facility. It was going to be competition for the only other long term care facility in our town. I knew there was a great need for the services we would provide because there was an extremely long waiting list at the other facility. It took some people years to gain entrance into that nursing care center.

So with determination and twenty years of nursing experience to my credit I began to work for P T I. The most interesting thing about this group was that the CEO and several other board members were Black. Yes I said Black! This blew my mind! Black men involved in health care at the top level! This was unheard of! This was their baby and I was going to be part of it.

You see Lompoc, Santa Maria, Arroyo Grande, Santa Barbara and especially Montecito; these cities are not known for having many Black residents much less Black owned businesses. There was a time when Lompoc had a hand full of Black owned businesses but there were only a few left now. You do not see Blacks in leadership in this region. It is possible that this is because of the demographics of our area but I don't believe it is the only reason. The time I spent at the Gardens helped to solidify my opinions on this matter.

Until we opened there was no need for a full staff. As construction came to an end they hired a maintenance manager and a business manager. Scott the maintenance man came with the building. Robin the business manager came from Santa Maria. The first order of business was to individually come up with a summation of what would be needed for our departments. We had no guidelines or budgets to work with. We had some supplies on hand and a few magazines from the most popular suppliers of health care products in the business and we had Bruce. Bruce was our advisor. I cannot recall his official title. I later came to call him the "Front Man". His job was to oversee things and get this project off the ground. Bruce was elderly. He had the look of an experienced man. He was a talker. He kind of reminded me of some ones grandfather. He looked distinguished with his white hair. For the record he was not a Black man. He was White.

Immediately I began to wonder about Bruce. One of the assignments he was supposed to accomplish was to relocate the supplies we had outside in a trailer and inventory them. He was a good talker but he didn't get much done. Then he hired the Dietary Manager and the Receptionist. Now I knew we had problems! The Dietician had no prior long- term care experience. She was a manager of a local restaurant he'd met while dining out one day. The receptionist also had no previous long-term care experience. She came for her interview dressed like she was going to or coming from the beach and she had a child with her during her interview. I could see the lust in his eyes as he proudly announced that she would be joining our team. It was clear to me he hired her for what she did for his male ego, not for what she had to offer the company. To top this off he began to tell me DONs had no involvement in the day-to-day operations of health care facilities. He declared that this was the Administrators job. I wondered what planet he was from and thought he should return home sometime real soon! While it was true that the Administrator is responsible for the day-to-day operations of a facility, the DON held the responsibility for the Nursing Department and the Resident's care. The nursing department is the largest department in any skilled care nursing facility. The DON and the Administrator are the ones who stand to jeopardize their professional license if or when things go wrong. I did not argue with him. I just concluded that he was ignorant concerning the health care business.

It was soon apparent that none of the PTI staff knew much about the health care industry. I began to hear things. We began to worry. In spite of this, things were going OK. They brought in an Administrative Consultant. His name was Bob. His presence alone provided some level of comfort for us when he was there.

I began to meet with suppliers and began researching and establishing contracts for services we would need. We needed Pharmacy services, Linen, Medical Equipment, Physical Therapy and Occupational Services, Activity Supplies and Hazardous Waste Management services. We would need a manager for Housekeeping, Social Services, Activities and a DSD. I had to prioritize and develop a plan for each phase of growth. What could we accomplish with the least amount of staff? When did it have to be done? We needed Policy and Procedure Manuals. We needed resource manuals like Physicians Desk References, PDRs and drug books. We needed refrigerators. We would need staff. The staff would need schedules and systems to work within. The list went on and on.

We got phones and computers. Things began to take shape.

Robin and I worked well together. We'd worked in one of the same facilities before working together this time. She had a horror story to tell. I had some horror stories to tell. She appeared to me to be a professional. We were all under great stress to perform. Most of this stress came from our own desire to succeed. But it was still stress never the less. Occasionally Robin was snippy. I attributed it to the stress of our situation. One of my goals was to build a team. I felt we were a team so I did not think too much of her snippiness. For the record Robin was White.

Then Bruce hired Mary. Mary was to be the Housekeeping Supervisor and Central Supply Manager. Mary came with experience in both areas and a work ethic I greatly admired. She was warm and friendly. She walked with authority. Mary was Hispanic. If I needed something done Mary would get it done.

In case you are wondering why I said if I needed something done she'd do it? That is because I was also acting as the Interim Administrator. It was cost effective for me as the DON to fulfill this role until we got closer to opening the facility. One of the first assignments I gave Mary was to take over Bruce's job of organizing and completing the inventory of the supplies we had on hand. There were bandages, gauze, urinals, wheelchairs, walkers, thermometers, you name it, we had some of it. Mary took care of this task with out blinking an eye.

Sam was the CEO. He was a family man. He was a nice man. He was a Black man. When Sam came to see how things were coming along he commented about the Central Supply room saying, I've been trying to get Bruce to organize those supplies for months. You guys did it within days! That was what Mary brought to the table.

Bob came to see us a few times. Things seemed to be on track. We started getting paid.

My employment began in June of 2001. It was now August 2001.

On August 12th I had this dream.

Me and husband going some place

Dressed up

I had a nice off white/ivory outfit on

We stopped at the Gardens (my job) on the way out.

Upon arrival noticed front of building being changed.

Scaffolds and construction going on

Men working

Noticed Terry coming out of building. She was looking for me.

I told her to wait for me so I could schedule an appointment with her. When I arrived at my office it was disheveled. I had trouble finding my things (? You don't belong there) I finally just grabbed a pocket-sized calendar and went out. Leaving my office, I also saw Robin. She left to go do something else. I wanted to ask her what was going on. I was very frustrated and upset that no one told me about the changes that were going on

(couldn't ask Robin) When I reentered front lobby things had been changed around and offices relocated.

Lots of commotion and people moving around. Terry now resting in her truck. Her husband got her attention

I saw personal things about her relationship with her husband

(She was recovering from some illness)

She was dressed in black/red? Plaid skirt and top with black velvet type shoes, flat, and loafer style

We tried to set up an appointment

. . . .

. . . . .

(Something that is coming. ? 3 months)

By this time dreams were a regular part of my nightlife. I was keeping a journal because I came to realize that my dreams gave me valuable insight into situations that were going to happen in my life and other people that I knew. Keep this one in mind.

Construction was completed we were full swing in what I thought was phase one of the the Gardens project. Bruce was now mostly available by phone. We didn't see Sam as much either. We had a few concerns about the inexperienced staff but overall we were making things work.

The next thing I knew we were getting phone calls from the light company and the gas company requesting payment for past due bills. Payroll checks began to bounce. They made them good and were able to make payroll the next time but now we were all nervous about the status of the company. When payday rolled around again the checks did not come in at all. Because I was in charge I called the main office. It was somewhere in southern California. I left message after message. I called Bruce. I got no response. I called every number I had. When I reached Sam he gave us hope. He explained they were experiencing some financial difficulties. I understood that things like this could happen so we hung in there. Then I couldn't get anyone to return my calls. I didn't know what to do. The staff looked to me for answers. Someone advised us to wait it out. If you leave you may never get paid. So we continued business as usual. After about three weeks I called the owner of the building. PTI was leasing the building. I told him what was going on. Within a short period of time he found someone else who was interested in purchasing the business from PTI. By this time we'd lost our receptionist but that was ok by me. Now Robin, Mary, Scott and I would share the responsibility of presenting the business to the potential new owners. My advice to them was that we compile all of our data. Organize it. And present the picture of what we've accomplished so far. If they decided to buy we wanted to keep our jobs. Therefore we needed to show them that we were valuable.

When it came time for the meetings the building was clean and we were prepared. Sam came for this meeting. He had to disclose the financial status of the business. That included the assets as well as the debts. When all was said and done The Gardens had new owners. We were excited again! We still had our jobs! Thank You Jesus!

By this time we had gone without pay for at least thirty days. By the time the take over was complete we were all hurting financially. The dietary manager left with PTI and things were off to a fresh new start. Thus my dream was fulfilled in part. The construction being done in the front of the building represented the face of the company being changed. Things were going to be totally rearranged and they were.

October 1, 2001, was my official new hire date. Bill, Kitty and Joyce were the new owners. They were a husband and wife team from Seattle Washington and Joyce was their partner. Although they had no health care experience or background, they assured us that they had the means and the backing to see this project through to fruition. After what we'd just been through I was concerned about the financial stability of their team too.

As I said they presented a good picture to us. They even gave us a sign on bonus because they felt bad about what we'd been through. I liked Bill. He presented himself to be a man of business. He came in with his lawyers and accountants. He had connections. He was fatherly and he had a sense of humor. He assured me "If you have any problems or concerns you just come to me". Kitty was nice. She was quiet and kind. She appeared to me to be more of a support person than a mover or shaker. Bill was the mover and the shaker. Joyce, Joyce was very particular. She had a very reserved way about her. She didn't smile much. She, according to Bill was being groomed for big business. They all had something to offer so they were indeed a team.

After taking care of the preliminary things such as redoing applications and I-9 forms for tax deductions we moved on to bigger things. I was still in charge of overall productivity. They provided more oversight by being on site. Meetings were held to monitor our progress. Things were looking good. Joyce was in charge of furnishing and decorating the building. Kitty was in charge of overseeing progress toward compliance for licensing. Bill was the mover and the shaker.

Knowing how regulated the long-term care business is. I immediately made copies of the Title 22 regulations for each of them. I thought they should know what they'd gotten themselves into. This was the guideline I was going by. I'd already given copies to the other staff members we had on board and felt the owners should know what we were doing too.

I had some concerns because they still did not give me a budget to work from and our new owners were totally ignorant about the type of business we were in. I also noticed that as soon as the new owners came into the picture, Robin distanced her self from me. She was no longer snippy at times. She was that way all the time. She didn't want to be bothered with me any more. This change was not gradual or subtle it was abrupt. It was as though she was saying I had to put up with you before but now I don't so don't bug me. I don't think she liked taking orders from me a Black nurse. I actually think she despised it but was cleaver enough to pretend that she was a team player until she no longer had to be.

Things were moving right along. Supplies were coming in. The rooms were being furnished. I was developing the Education Department, the Nursing Department, the Activities Department, the Social Services Department, the Medical Records Department and researching the needs for the Alzheimer's unit. It was now December.

Bill hired a Chef to manage the kitchen and another Maintenance Manager to oversee Scott. Steve had no health care background but he had maintenance experience.

Mary hired Lilly. I hired Albertah as the DSD and I hired the Medical Director so he would be on board when it came time to do the employee physicals.

Albertah was an interesting individual. I clearly remember looking at her resume and being impressed with her background. When I called her about her resume I felt a connection to her as though we had something in common. When she came for her interview I was pleasantly surprised to see she was Black. Usually I can tell by a person's voice what nationality they are. I did not say always. I said usually. In this case I couldn't tell. She had a lot of experience in nursing. She was well groomed. The only problem was that her experience was not in California.

Bill was not willing to advertise for help, nor was he willing to pay wages that were comparable to those of other facilities in our area. We had a tentative date set for our licensing survey so I felt she was the best candidate for the position. I needed Albertah to be ready and able to orientate the rest of the new employees when they came on board so I started her training right away. I was looking forward to taking off one of my hats. I was wearing more hats than I wanted to be wearing. The sooner I could focus solely on the Nursing Department the better I would feel!

During the training we hit it off well. She was very knowledgeable so I didn't have to go overboard with my explanations and expectations. I'd ordered most of the supplies. The classroom was furnished. I just needed someone qualified to take over. Other than age, we seemed to have a lot in common. She was at least twenty years older than I was. She was what I call seasoned. She told me how impressed she was to meet me. I was the first Black DON she'd seen in California. As we talked she began to tell me things about my life I knew she could not have known. She said, "Words cannot express the price that you have paid to be here in this position today". People don't know what you've been through to get here. She asked, have you ever thought about writing a book? I explained that I desired years ago to write a book about my life but had long since forgotten about that desire. With the changes that had occurred in my life over the years I never had the time to do it. She then told me, the Lord is going to put you in a situation that will allow you the time to write your book. The thing that was interesting about this encounter was that I felt a mixture of affirmation and distrust concerning her words to me. This was how our relationship started and ended. It was riddled with confusion. One minute I felt she was in my corner. The next minute I felt I could not trust her.

Robin hired Willene, a Black woman to be our Admissions Coordinator. Steve the Chef hired Derrick a young Black man to assist him in the kitchen. Suddenly the face of this company was full of color. Blacks held three key positions, management positions at the Gardens. When I realized this I was pleasantly amazed. I had not seen this before and have not seen it since then.

I hired the initial nursing staff, one nurse for days, one for PM's and one for nights. I hired Terry for Medical Records. They were all white.

She was the Terry who was in my dream. I had not seen her for years. We'd worked at the local hospital in the ER together. She applied for a job with us. After greeting her I told her I had a dream about her very recently. I told her the contents of the dream. After listening to me she confirmed that the things I saw in the dream were true! Very interesting! We wondered what this meant (hum)

We were preparing for the first orientation of our new staff. Soon we had each key player hired and scheduled for orientation. This included my new boss Janice and my daughter who Janice hired to be an assistant to the Activities Director. I was thrilled to finally be in a position to help someone in my family get ahead in the work force. In my experience, Blacks don't usually get the hook up. I never did. Now I was able to help my daughter pursue her interest. She would not be in the nursing department so Janice felt she'd be perfect for the position.

Initially I'd recommended her for the receptionist position. She was articulate, well dressed, creative and her eyes lit up any room she entered. Bill and Kitty did not want her in that position. They never really told me why. I was naïve. I actually thought I had some clout with the Sperry's. I later realized they didn't want a Black face representing their company. I let my daughter know up front that she would be held to a higher standard than the others on staff just like I would. It was important to me that she knew what to expect. This was something I had to learn on my own. We were nervous but excited! We had each other. I was not alone this time.

Orientation day came. I stayed late the night before making sure we were prepared. I planned to conduct the first day of training. I wanted to set the stage. Albertah would conduct the second day of training for the nursing staff. The other managers would continue the remainder of the training needed for their staff and so on. The classroom was full. Robin was to make an appearance to represent her department, the business department. Janice was to make an appearance so the staff would know who was in charge of the overall operations of the facility.

Now Janice was a middle aged attractive White lady. She was a brunette with a pretty smile. She came to us with good recommendations. She had been an

Administrator for around five years but only had a few years of actual on the job experience. The owners interviewed one other candidate that they were not pleased with. Again, Bill did not want to advertise for this position so we agreed she would probably be the best person for this position under the circumstances. Like Robin was at first, Janice was very nice. I showed her what we'd accomplished so far. We seemed to hit it off. It seemed that we had a similar vision for our facility. We both wanted to provide excellent care. I was in the process of building a team and she expressed that she was in agreement with this concept.

Back to orientation day, shortly after reviewing our history/origin, organizational structure and mission statements I introduced Janice. It was time for her to meet the staff, our team. My mouth fell to the floor when she let us all know in no pleasant terms that she was in charge! If you didn't like it, there is the door! She said. She did not crack a smile. What was she doing? This is not the way you build a team! I was shocked! This was not the same smiling women I'd been interacting with. She was cold. She was abrupt and she told us if we wanted to keep our jobs we'd better recognize who was in control.

At some point Robin made her appearance. She was upset about having to speak to the staff. She also made this point very clear. Without ever removing her coat she in a very monotone voice explained her role to the staff. If I paraphrase what she said I'd say it like this. I'm Robin. I work in the business office but I hope you don't ever bother me. In one fail swoop the two of them threw my team concept out the window. I could feel the tension in the room. Willene was openly offended with Robin's behavior she and other staff members began to ask me confrontational questions after Janice and Robin left. It was apparent they felt threatened. It was also apparent that this was what Janice and Robin now close buddies wanted. They were in charge now. Like it or leave. I smoothed things over as much as I could by completing the orientation in a professional manner.

At the end of the day I instinctively knew we were in for big trouble. Now I was anxious in a negative way. I was very disappointed with the way Robin presented her department. I, thinking Janice and I still had somewhat of a rapport, told Janice how I felt about it. I was technically still acting as the Administrator until Janice training was complete. We, I thought, were the only ones left in the building when I discussed the matter with her. To my surprise Robin came walking into the room. She'd been there long enough to hear my concerns and she did not like it! She immediately complained to Joyce about me. Joyce corrected me for talking about the matter in a public area instead of behind closed doors but instructed me that

I should talk with Robin personally. She confirmed my observations by letting me know that Robin complained to them about being asked to do the presentation. But they told her she needed to do it any way. I accepted Joyce's correction and advice. I called Robin at home that night. She didn't like that either! "Why do you think you have the right to say anything about my performance"? She yelled! I have every right to critique your performance. I replied. I was the one who asked you to give it. It was for the Education Department of which I am still involved in and I am still in charge until Janice completes her training! We went back and forth. I acknowledged to her that I should have discussed the matter in private even though I thought we were alone but maintained that her presentation was very unprofessional. From that point on she despised me. After all, who was I, a Black woman, to tell her anything? My titles didn't matter to her. She literally cringed any time I came into the room after that discussion. (Another part of the dream fulfilled) I could not talk with Robin any more.

Shortly after this I completed Janice's orientation and turned all of my contracts over to her. These would now be areas she would be responsible for. I wanted her to be comfortable. She took over the facility preparations for licensure. She was very comfortable taking over and I was glad to be relieved of my extra responsibilities.

She continued to educate the owners. She conducted stand up meetings on a daily basis to review progress. I thought maybe things would be all right after all. She brought another level of structure and organization to the table. This was impressive. Now that Janice was in place I could focus wholeheartedly on the nursing department, my department, my baby. So that is what I did.

It was the month of December. As the holiday approached I showed my appreciation to the staff for the hard work they did by giving out bottles of Sparkling Apple Cider, a favorite of mine. I don't drink alcohol.

We had our first Christmas party. We celebrated with delicacies made in our very own kitchen. It was a gourmet style kitchen and we had a gourmet Chef also named Steve. It was a good opportunity to break the kitchen in. It was perfect. I received gifts from our vendors. Although it was customary I appreciated it and it made me feel special. It made some people feel jealous.

We hired a pianist. He was an acquaintance I knew and recommended from Montecito. We invited our family members. My husband came with me. Bill seemed to really like him. They both retired from the military and had things in common.

Joyce and I sang Christmas Carols together. She even requested a special number from me. It was one I'd sung when we'd traveled on a business trip together not to long before. She was fond of it so I sang it for her. The night went well.

December 26th came. Ironically it was also my Birthday. It was time for my three-month evaluation. I'd worked very hard up to this point and I hoped my evaluation would reflect my efforts. I didn't trust people the way I used too. Bill, Kitty and Joyce did the evaluations. To my relief my meeting went well. I got a very good performance evaluation. My status was changed to salaried and I was promised a raise effective March 1, 2002.

The one thing I did not like was hearing that we would be revaluated in 3 more months to assure them we were continuing to perform at an acceptable level. Janice would do the next evaluations. This would give her more time to observe our performance. I understood that the owners had no previous health care experience so they wanted to rely on Janice for her input but they did have management experience so I smelled a rat. Something just didn't feel right about this.

Janice was temporarily in charge of marketing and the bosses wanted to have a ribbon cutting ceremony and an open house to alert the public of our presence in the community. Janice was already frustrated. One day she shared some of her concerns with me about working with the owners and her wages. My mistake, I listened and confirmed that she was extremely generous to agree to work for them for such a low wage. She didn't know they would ask her to do marketing too! She came to me for advice. She'd never done anything like that before. I assured her I had experience with performing and putting on shows and hosting events, not to worry I would help her.

I assisted her with the plans. We would need to decide which guest we wanted to come. Our invites would go to Doctors, vendors, families of residents on waiting list, other Facilities, the Chamber of Commerce and so on. Each manager was asked to provide a list of those they wanted to invite. We would need Horsderves. Willene would provide tours of the facility. Each manager would be assigned to specific areas for example when Willene brought them to me I would discuss the services we would offer in the Nursing Department. It really was one of my easier assignments.

When the date of the open house came all was ready. This would be a long day but it was exciting. My excitement quickly turned to sorrow. When the Camber of Commerce arrived for the publicity photos and the ribbon cutting ceremony, Janice was called to the forefront. She was introduced as the new Administrator. They smiled and took pictures for the newspaper. The owners never bothered to introduce me. I was hurt but maintained my professionalism. Of course the Chamber representatives were all White. I could see the distain in their eyes as they looked at me as though I didn't belong there. It was a familiar look. One that said we can't say what we are thinking but we would if we could. They didn't even know I was the DON. I got the feeling the Sperry's didn't want them to know either. I went home crushed that night. Not only did they treat me that way but several of the local DON's from local facilities came to our open house. They also looked at me with distain as if looking down their noses at me like, how did you get this position?

The one I remember vividly was a DON from Santa Maria. Her name was Debbie. To this day I cringe when I remember her nasty disposition towards me. I'd lived in Lompoc for a long time so I knew lots of people in the business. I knew of Debbie. When she came to my building she could barely muster up a fake smile. The place was beautiful. We had beautiful antiques and furnishings. I was not supposed to be a part of this. It was too much for her prejudiced mindset to conceive of.

Some of my previous work acquaintances were very proud and supportive of me. Albertah told me you can't trust them (Whites). "That is why I don't socialize with them out side of work". She did not come to the open house. I didn't want that to be true but felt deeply in my heart it was true in this case. I later learned that I could not trust Albertah either but I will explain that later on in my story.

I began to distrust the owners at this point. This opened my eyes to other things as well. I thought I was appreciated and respected by them but I was really just cheap labor. I laid the foundation for them. That was good but they made it clear they would take it from here.

Things went from bad to worse. It was now January. Janice became unpredictable. She gave me permission to attend a DSD meeting in Santa Barbara to do some networking. When I returned she was upset with me for going to the meeting. She was scheduled to meet with the Medical Director and didn't like the fact that I wasn't there to hold her hand during the meeting. Albertah told me you should go and talk with her about this. I refused to suck up to her unstable ways. She'd given me permission to go. I was not going to apologize for going. She was the boss. She should be able to get through one meeting without me. I'd handled much more than that all by myself.

Later I requested a few days off to attend a spiritual conference in Anaheim. It was wonderful! When I returned I was refreshed and radiant. Janice saw this. She appeared angry about it. She seemed like a baby having a tantrum and told me "we'll see what we can do to wipe that smile off your face"! It seemed again as though she felt abandoned, like she was saying how dare you go off, have fun and leave me here to manage things all by myself! I was stunned. She hadn't needed me for the open house publicity photos, did she? She was vicious when she wanted to be and interestingly so, so insecure (hum).

The staff began to express concerns to me. It was getting closer to time for our inspection for licensing. Janice was supposed to be training some of the staff for special duties. They were not getting trained. The communication was breaking down. When they tried to talk with Janice they too faced her wrath. I referred them to Janice any way for guidance. I did not want to step on her toes. Finally I agreed to share their concerns with Janice. I reported that a few of the staff had some concerns about when they would be receiving the training they were promised. They expressed they wanted to be ready for survey. To this she angrily asked me "Why are they coming to you? If they have a problem they need to come to me. I am the boss!" Seeing she was upset I agreed with her telling her I think they come to me because they were used to doing that before she came but I know my place and will handle the situation however you would like for me to handle it. I am simply passing the message on to you. She continued to explode! From now on if they have a problem, they need to come to me! It was clear she was taking her frustrations out on me so I confronted her about it and asked her what she would prefer me to do in the future if I learn of a problem? I reassured her that she was the boss. She did not need to be concerned about that. I was just trying to keep the lines of communication open!

So much for maintaining the lines of communication, she was offended. That was all there was to it! Go figure. She alienated the staff from her with her dictator's attitude. Now she did not like the response she provoked. The mature thing to do would have been to acknowledge her mistake. Evaluate her approach and try again. She wasn't going to do that. She had too much pride for that. My Bible tells me that pride always goes before a fall. I believe that to be true.

From that point on she began to distance her self from me. She purposefully withheld information from me so when the staff was confused so was I. In spite of this I continued to communicate my needs and status to her as usual. She stopped responding to my memo's and phone messages. How can you work for some one that you are accountable to who will not talk to you? This was my new dilemma.

We hosted another open house. This time Janice planned it. We were no longer a team. She was effective with intimidating the rest of the staff into place. They were afraid to talk to me now and they were afraid to talk to her. When it came time for the entertainment plans Bill wanted me to sing again. I respectfully declined his request. I had no song in my spirit that I wanted to share with them. It was painfully apparent that we did not share the same type of relationship I thought we had in the beginning. I wasn't going to be the Black entertainment for the Masters this time.

I began to distance myself as well. I had a lot of work to do in the Nursing Department any way. May be giving her space would decrease her insecurities concerning me.

My stocked medications came in and I needed to inventory them and arrange them. I buried myself in my work often to the point that I didn't even realize when lunchtime came and went. I got used to taking late lunches so that I would not have to eat alone in a room even though other staff members were there. I was salaried so it didn't matter any way. At least I thought it didn't matter.

One-day maintenance Steve came to me when I was working in the supply room. He asked me was there a problem between Janice and me. Not wanting to fan any flames, I told him no, at least not on my end of the spectrum. I explained to him that I felt the dynamics of our team have changed drastically and I am just trying to find my place within the changes. He expressed his concern that he'd noticed a change in my behavior and approach to situations in our meetings. He confirmed and agreed that things had really changed and tried to encourage me.

January 19th 2002 I wrote in my dream journal:

................*Now in a new area, can't remember surroundings.*

Suddenly a woman soldier appeared. She was a black woman, a foreigner; she had braids in her hair. She started yelling at me. There were others with me but I can't remember who they were. The soldier started chewing me out. I didn't know what she was talking about, she was getting upset because I wasn't responding the way she wanted me to. I couldn't understand her instructions even though she was speaking English. She warned me that she was going to leave for a few days. When she came back I had better do what she told me to do. I didn't fully understand but somehow she was telling me to get ready to be shipped out. They were trying to send me somewhere.

A few others, and myself I didn't seem to know, were with me. We began trying to clean up the place................... I knew she was on her way back so I tried to separate my pictures from my personal identification. I felt I should give my pictures to my friends who were with me and keep my ID on me. I placed it in my pocket just in case we got separated. I knew they were trying to take me away!

A week later I was crushed. One day I went to the kitchen to get my meal for lunch. Our meals were free. Steve the Chef told Derrick not to serve me. I asked why? He didn't know so he went and asked Steve why, at my request. Steve very gruffly told me through him, it is a new rule! What new rule I asked? He stated Bill told him if I did not come for lunch at noon I was not to be served! I asked, when was this rule made? Was it given in a memo? How was this rule communicated? He did not know but he refused to serve me. I felt humiliated. I was the DON, second in charge of this facility and they refused to serve me lunch. No one bothered to tell me this new information. I would have complied.

I felt like I was experiencing the discrimination of the sixties. No Blacks aloud! We do not serve darkies. White only pies! I felt sick to my stomach and suddenly lost my appetite. I signed out for lunch and went home. The more I thought about it the more it bothered me. This was the last straw! This was a direct attack against me and for what?

In the past Bill told me if I had any problems, do not hesitate to come to him so I decided to go to him. You'd think I'd learned by now that this would do no good. I hadn't. I still believed in following protocol. Bill was the next line of communication above Janice. Protocol says if you cannot resolve a problem with your immediate supervisor go up the chain until you get resolution.

I was truly distraught. My spirit was crushed. From home I called Bill. I informed

evident in the facility between Janice and myself as a result of our word exchange. He voiced his understanding and expressed he was not aware the problems I presented to him existed. I emphasized to him I was concerned about the confusion, the lack of communication and hoped we could resolve it. I did not feel I should focus on my personal feelings. He told me to take the rest of the day off. He assured me he would get to the bottom of things and get back to me later that day. I waited by the phone. He never called me back. Now I had a very uneasy feeling in my gut.

As I prepared for work the next morning I felt a sense of doom. I felt like I was in a fog and was moving in slow motion as though I was detached from myself. It was January 26th, 2002. Something was dreadfully wrong!

During stand up Janice asked me a few questions but I deflected them to the persons over the areas she was asking about so as not to allow her to put me on the spot and the department heads could answer for them selves. After the meeting she asked me to stay behind. I thought she wanted to talk to me about my concerns from the day before. She asked Steve the maintenance manager to stay behind as well. This puzzled me. Then she asked, "You expressed some concerns to Bill yesterday"? Yes I did. "Well I thought Bill was going to be here for this meeting but I guess he's not". Pause. So we've decided to relieve you of your responsibilities! She was very direct and to the point. I was literally stunned. For a moment I was speechless. After I composed my thoughts I could only reply, "Yes maam". Mockingly I stood up to leave. I saw her flinch as though she thought I was going to reach for her. This puzzled me for a moment. Why would she expect me to hurt her? I forgot. I was Black. That meant I could be dangerous. We have been known to go off you know! She handed my check to me and asked Steve to personally escort me to my office to gather my belongings and then escort me out of the building. Still in a daze I walked to my office. Once I arrived there I thought for a moment I was going to go crazy! My thoughts were racing. I wanted to destroy my office! All of the work I'd done! We were so close to inspection! Why were they doing this to me? I couldn't grasp what was happening to me.

Suddenly I composed my thoughts. I told Steve I am not some type of criminal. You do not have to guard me as though I'm dangerous. I could see he was also stunned and confused. We'd worked well together. He agreed with me and told me to take all the time I needed. I felt compassion for him. I felt he was caught off guard too.

Then my emotions went from anger, to containment, to shame and humiliation. I just wanted to get my things and get out of there. I wanted to hide my head in shame and I didn't want any one to see me leave. **But the Lord spoke to my spirit**

and said, no you don't! You will leave out the front door just the way you came in. You have not done anything to be ashamed of so do not hang your head in shame!

So that is what I did. I collected my belongings and I marched right out the front door. On the way I saw Willene and several other staff members. They asked me what was going on? I told them I'd been fired. They began to openly weep and cry.

I put my belongings in my trunk and asked Steve for permission to go back inside. He replied "Diane I don't know what is going on so you can do whatever you want to do". So I went back inside.

I went to the conference room where I found Robin, Janice and Albertah. I let Robin know I knew she didn't care for me but I wished her the best anyhow. I told her I was just trying to do my job and do it well. With a partial smirk she denied that she ever had a problem with me. Next I said goodbye to Albertah. She looked very upset too. She asked me for a hug. I hesitated to give her one at first because she was near Janice and I did not want to get close to Janice. After looking Janice in the eyes, I gave Albertah a goodbye hug. Later that day Albertah told me Janice cried after I left the conference room. Make sense of that if you can. I couldn't.

Then I went to the corporate office were I found Bill, Kitty and Joyce. They looked up in surprise when they saw me. I said, I don't know what reason I was sent here but I must have completed my assignment. As a Christian I believe everything happens for a reason. I told them "thank you for the opportunity you gave me to work here." I thought they'd just decided I wasn't mature enough for the position or something like that. Bill mumbled under his breath, what a remarkable woman. I sensed he was astonished by my response. Kitty gave me a hug telling me I'd done a good job and that was the way I left the Gardens, wounded but with my head held high.

I did not know why I was fired but resolved within myself that they were the experienced ones in business, not this business, but maybe they had reasons I could not see. I was soon to learn this was not the case at all.

After learning what had happened to me my daughter quit. But our former employer was not going to let them mess over my child. I agreed to go to the facility with her to resolve the matter. Before we even got to the front door Joyce came out to impede our progress. She was smug and prissy looking as usual but more so today. She asked may I help you? I replied no thank you, we just came to get my daughters last paycheck. She resigned but has not received her final paycheck. She very offensively told me "Diane you know you are not allowed in the building and your daughter never worked here so why don't you just leave!" To that I became indignant! Excuse me! My daughter attended orientation training with Miss Albertah and myself. She was working with Alicia in the Activities Department and you owe her for those days of training and work! Further more what is with the attitude? Have I done something to offend you? She sarcastically replied, you should know! I should know what I asked? She went on to tell me the lies Janice told them about me to cover her butt. "You lied on your application about your experience. You were stirring up trouble with the staff causing confusion. You ordered supplies we did not need. You should have known it would catch up to you"! To this my daughter became offended because Joyce was now in my face and was being condescending. She stopped her, look here! My mother might let you talk to her that way but I will not allow it! I am not nice like her so you better watch your step! What are you acting scared for? We are not gonna hurt you but you better act like you have some sense! Joyce backed up. She appeared a bit shaken. Perhaps she'd heard or assumed we, Blacks, could act a fool when provoked. I responded to her accusations. That is a total fabrication! Where did you get this information? I do not lie! I am a Minister of the gospel of Jesus Christ and I love him with all my heart! I would not lie. I did not lie on my application or Resume! Every word of it is true! Janice was the one who checked my references after I told her she had to and showed her how to do it so she could complete my file! I showed her how to verify my nursing license, which she did! If you guys had any doubts all you had to do was call the State Board and check my references. They could verify when I became an RN and where I worked before! I ordered supplies based on my knowledge and background. You guys did not give me any guidelines or a budget to work from and further more, this is not what you said about me in the evaluation you gave me only a month ago! As far as me stirring up trouble with the staff, the staff came to me for help. I just delivered the message to Janice for them! No one else was bold enough to push the issue with Janice! She replied. You know we did not know what we were doing! At that point I knew it was fruitless to say anything more to her about my situation. They did not even have the decency to stand by their own evaluation of me. I now knew why I was fired. Janice lied! She was more of a witch than I thought. It was painfully clear. Janice had only been there less than a month. I had twenty years of nursing experience. She only had a few years but all she had to do was put on her White face and lie. Just like that they believed her. I think this is what hurt me the most. They were going to stick together no matter what.

I changed the subject. I didn't even come here to talk about me. I came to help my daughter out. You can get away with mistreating me but I will not let you cheat her!

Now she changed her tune. Diane I will check into the matter for you and get to the bottom of the problem. You can trust me. I've always been reliable with you. That was before! I said! That was before you fired me without a cause, without even investigating on my behalf. Everything you needed was right in my file. Now trying not to break down I told her I trusted you guys! We went to dinner together. We invited you to our home etc. etc. She reassured me she would take care of the matter so we left.

It turned out that Robin did not have the proper tax form on file for my daughter. That was why she had not gotten paid. At this point the facility was not open. We were only operating with a small-scale staff and their lack of competence was already apparent to me. Little Miss Attitude had not completed the needed paper work. Janice sent my daughter a letter with this explanation and the form Robin needed. She filled it out and they mailed the check out to her.

What they did not know was that prayer changes things! While I was working for PTI, I had walked through that whole building praying for the success of the facility. Lord let it be a place where patients and staff a like will feel special, where people can receive healing. Let us stand out in the community as a place where people really care about people. Make us a model. But Lord, if it will not bring you glory, do not let it be! I claimed that territory for Gods Kingdom!

The way things turned out it seemed as though I was the one who was defeated. My dream had come true. The soldier lady did not just want to send me away. She got rid of me. Have you ever experienced a time when you trusted God for something and it turned out totally different then you expected? Did it leave you confused and your faith shaken? If so I can relate!

Now I wanted to sue them! I wanted to make them pay for the pain and humiliation they caused me but the Lord said no. He impressed in my spirit, that action would not show them His love. So I did not sue.

attack against me that it wounded my spirit. I battled with the feeling that I was a failure. I asked myself why over and over? I searched myself trying to find an answer that would soothe me. Did I do something wrong? May be I should have done this or that. For six months I grieved the loss of that job. This time I didn't hyperventilate though. The day it happened, I drove myself home. I called and told my husband what happened. He offered to come right home. I told him he did not need to. I would be ok.

I thank the Lord for a loving and supportive husband. I thank him for his word the Bible. I thank him for the time I'd already spent getting to know about him because that is what carried me through this devastating ordeal. The word of God says bless them that curse you. Pray for them that spitefully use you so that is what I did in the midst of my struggle.

Not once now but two times in less than a year, I'd been fired for doing a good job to cover up some one else that was doing a poor work.

As I began to heal, I realized I'd given it my best shot. I was not a Politician nor was I a faker. I would not do anything different if I had the chance to do it over again. This allowed me to see them for who they really were. Sometimes that is just the way it is. People are evil. I some how found strength in knowing that I still did not compromise to fit in with the crowd. It was obvious to me that Janice felt threatened by me and she was not the type of person to share the spot light with any one else. We had totally different management styles and values. There was no way we could have become a team. She'd made it clear during orientation that it was her way or the highway so I should have expected it.

It is truly an honor to be mistreated for rightness sake. I maintained my identity. That was the final portion of my dream.

I placed my identification in my pocket to keep it with me just in case we got separated.

I'd worked since I was seventeen. I'd never had any real leisure time off for myself. It was very hard for me to adjust to this at first. I did not know what to do with myself. I'd been knocked off my horse. I was traumatized so I did not want to get back on my horse any time soon but I wasn't used to not working. I felt guilty about not working.

The first few weeks were the worse. After a few more, I began to realize there were lots of things I'd wanted to do but hadn't had the time to do. After complaining to my husband about this several times he encouraged me to enjoy my new found freedom while I could so I did. I began to exercise again. I went jogging. I unpacked boxes that we still had in our garage from 2000 when my husband retired form the US Air force. I did some decorating and reorganizing in my home. I created an office for myself and a dressing room for my husband. Our children were gone at that time. My husband kept telling me we were free now, so enjoy it! I began to do just that. I'd never had the privilege of being a stay home mom. Now I was home with out my kids. That was even better.

A few months later I was doing some things around the house when I heard the Spirit of the Lord tell me to write. I instinctively knew it was now time for me to write the story of my painful child hood and very painful first marriage. I recognized that this was the situation that Albertah told me would happen so I would have time to write my book. It was long over due. I didn't know that Albertah would play a part in my departure.

After I left the Gardens we talked on the phone often. She pretended to care about my misfortune. She kept me informed of what was going on back at the Gardens.

One night I had a dream about her. I saw her tiptoeing around the halls of the Gardens dressed like a Ninja warrior. I told her of this dream. It was puzzling to me. It was as though she was some type of spy. My husband told me. Be careful. She is a spy but she is a double agent.

Even though I didn't fully trust her, Albertah and I did develop a relationship. I didn't consider her to be a friend but I could say she was an associate. She professed to be a Missionary and we had similar beliefs in the Bible so I tried to maintain a relationship with her. I was raised to respect my elders and she was at least twenty years my senior so I gave her that respect.

Soon I began to hear things that Albertah supposedly said. Things she repeated to Janice that I'd told her. You see I'd lived in this community for a long time now. There were very few management jobs to be had. It was very important to me that I protected my reputation so I told the staff members I'd hired what happened to me after I left. I told them I was fired and why I was fired. I didn't want any lies tarnishing my reputation. I felt some embarrassment about being fired. But I was not ashamed for people to know the truth about what happened. We lived in a small town. It was bound to leak out to the nursing community that I was no longer working at the Gardens. I also felt responsible to the people I'd hired to let them one leave but I did tell my side of the story. If they chose to stay that would be on them. I told Albertah I'd done this. I heard she went back and told Janice what I'd done. I knew someone repeated this info to someone because Joyce mentioned it to me the day she confronted me in the parking lot with my daughter. Joyce didn't like it! She told me I should have kept my mouth shut about what happened. That way no one would have known. I told her it was my right to tell my side of the story and tell it I did.

I should not have been surprised that within weeks of my departure two more Black employees were gotten rid of. One was forced out. The other one was also fired. Albertah was the only one who managed to stay there for a while longer. I think she had more experience at playing the game (double agent). Several months later she told me she just didn't go back to work because things were so bad she couldn't take it. I would doubt that what she told me was true because of the source it came from but I know what finally happened to the Gardens. I'll tell you that later in my story.

Initially I did not think that my termination was race related but when I saw that the next three employees to be let go or leave the company after me were Black. I formed a new opinion. It later became apparent that the totality of the facilities problems were Bill, Kitty, Joyce and Janice but it was impossible to deny that race issues were a part of the whole mess. The Blacks were the first to go!

Any way, I now had time on my hands. When I sat down to write my story, the words just flowed from my mind to my keyboard. I remembered things that I had not thought about in years. I did not write it for healing but writing it brought another level of healing into my life. I'd been rejected and abused so many times and ways, that I had a deep-rooted fear of being rejected. I was able to see how much I'd grown when I accepted no blame for the way I was treated at the Gardens.

When you've been rejected and abused a lot you have a tendency to blame yourself when things go wrong. I learned through these job situations to evaluate myself. Make changes if I needed to and leave the rest alone. I could place the blame where it should be. I did not have to own it if it is was not mine to own. This was very liberating for me.

As I looked back over my life and saw it on paper I began to see how strong I was. I was a walking miracle. I consistently chose not to become bitter when others wronged me. It was not that I was strong in and of myself but through faith and obedience to Gods word I'd come a long ways. Earlier times in my life when my faith was tested I caved in. Now I knew I really believed what I preached and talked about. It was time to tell of my struggles and failures so that others could benefit form my experiences.

That is why I'm writing this story. I want others to benefit from my experiences. Although I experienced negative encounters in my career. I never compromised my integrity. Integrity is so valuable. There was a time when a person's word was their bond. I still believe this should be so. If you can't count on a person's word you can't trust them. My Granny used to tell us. If you'll lie, you will steal. If you will steal you will cheat. Believe it because it is true!

What you see is what you get when you encounter me. I am not pretentious or fake. I never learned how to play the political game. I did not want to and I pray you will not either. If you have compromised yourself in any way it is not to late to change.

Chapter 13

After four months I decided it was time to get back on my horse. I decided to do some Consulting. That was something I'd never done. I worked a very short time for a group home in Santa Maria. They contracted my services. I was to do chart and medication reviews for their mentally disabled clients and train the staff. I was their QA person.

I don't have a whole lot to say about this experience except to say Albertah recommended this job to me. She did not bother to tell me she'd quit abruptly after being offended by the way her boss treated her. I can't even remember the woman's name. I just know she was rude and condescending towards me so I also quit abruptly.

I was not about to go through those types of changes with her or anyone else for that matter.

I could see the writing on the wall the day I had my interview. She was very complimentary of my red suit and physical presentation but said it in a way to let me know she felt underdressed, insecure at the time.

It didn't take me several years to conclude she had no integrity. She lied to me about the requirements of the job. "Oh, you hardly ever get calls or pages. I had the pager for two weeks and I only got one or two calls, she said." I was tied to a pager 24/7, morning noon and night. In a few months I'd received close to two hundred pages from the staff.

Then she had the nerves to call me one day and chew me out because one of her staff told her I did not respond to a page. She didn't know I was not stupid. I kept a log of every page I received by date and time. It included who I spoke to, what the problem was and how I'd resolved it. After taking care of her concern I investigated her accusation and found that I had called that person back twice. The person who called me was the one who did not return my call. On top of that, the person she'd left in charge did not know what she wanted and did not even give her the message that I'd called. We agreed the need must not have been that important. I explained this to the manager and she continued to defend her staff member telling me "You can explain your side to my staff in a meeting if you are not happy with what you are being accused of."

Let me remind you, I was the professional. I was the one with the License. Her staff team leader was a trained care provider off the street so to speak. She had no formal education but I was the one she wanted to explain or defend myself. I emphatically let her know I would not be attending any meeting to explain my self. I am telling you I've done my research. This is what happened! You need to investigate what happened on your end of the spectrum and get back to me. She did not want to do this. It was easier for her to chew me out then to think that one of her staff could cause such confusion. The boss continued to chew me out any way. Actually she was not even my boss. I was my own boss. I was contracted. I just needed to know what guidelines they needed me to work within. Other than that I was supposed to have full say over how I provided my services.

Long story short, I quit.

During this time I did some research to see if I could become a Nursing Home Administrator. I learned that I had the years of experience I needed to qualify. The qualification was ten years experience in Long-Term Care or possessing a Baccalaureate Degree. I just needed someone to precept me. I searched the entire Central Coast for that someone and came up with no one.

I talked with Albertah, my informant, about what I wanted to do. I was tired of working from the middle. If I was going to stay in nursing I wanted to work from the top. She encouraged me to pursue my desires but was glad to inform me that "maintenance" Steve at the Gardens was now being precepted by Janice to become an Administrator. Remember Steve had no prior medical background. He qualified because he had a degree of some kind. I had nothing against Steve on a personal level but I did have a problem with this "way of the World" system. It was in my face again blaring like a neon sign. Less qualified people getting promoted!!! "You scratch my back, I'll scratch yours," AKA "THE GOOD OLD BOY" system. In my opinion a degree does not qualify you to understand the intricacies of taking care of people. It will give you insight but it does not qualify you. I knew that from my own nursing education, my training was only a foundation from which I could build on.

This is why I believe in doing things Gods' way. In God's Kingdom, one gets promoted by what one does, how we use our gifts and talents and by being faithful to our calling. He does not promote you for reading the book, his book. He promotes you for living the book. He has no respect of persons. He will not promote you in life if you are not qualified and he will not cheat you out of anything in life if you are intended to have it. It would behoove the managers and leaders of the world systems and entities to understand this and do things God's way. The Bible tells servants (employees) and masters (employers) how they should interact with each other. It is ashamed for a servant to be slothful (lazy). And it is ashamed for a master to mistreat a servant. This implies there should be a mutual appreciation for each other.

I know that a wicked heart is full of jealousy, contention, anger, creates confusion and despises others because of its' own inadequacies. I know too that even if I had a degree Janice would never have precepted me. This meant I would have to return to nursing.

Nursing was not appealing to me at this point. Management was certainly not appealing to me that is, not as a DON. So I decided to go back to working the floor. This time it was in a different capacity. I applied to work at a place in Santa Barbara. It was a continuing care retirement community on the order of the facility in Montecito . They needed nurses to work in their clinic. So they hired me.

Chapter 14

In my interview I was very candid about my work experience. I talked openly about the things that occurred during my time at the Gardens. If they needed me it wouldn't matter. If it mattered this was not the job for me. That is how I felt. It didn't matter to Steve. Steve was my new boss. He had a few horror stories of his own that he was glad to share with me. He was also candied about some of his experiences.

He had no previous long term care experience. He was already overwhelmed with this new job. He had not been there that long. He told me he was thinking about quitting because the demands were so great.

You see, now the business had declined to the point that in some places the DON had to work the floor as charge nurse when needed even if you 'd already worked a full day. I'd been their too. This is not how it was the in the early days. Now they wanted you to do it all and be all things to everybody. The glamour was gone. No more days of sitting in the office while the rest of the staff did the dirty work. That was another reason I didn't really want to go into management as a DON again. I did not want to work crazy hours. I felt I'd paid my dues already. Opportunities were supposed to get better not worse with age and years of experience. But the rising cost of health care, fraud, waste and abuse and poor management had changed all of that.

To my surprise Steve even asked me if I would consider becoming the DON when and if he decided to leave. Thinking it might help secure this job, I told him I was open to the idea.

I was not used to the long hours any more. The work wasn't hard but the shifts were 12 hours. That was a big adjustment for me. I hadn't worked consistently as a floor nurse in five years. I adjusted though and found that I actually did still enjoy caring for people.

As a clinic nurse I provided emergency services and medication administration/oversight to our residents'. The resident's were in an "Assisted" level of care. Technically that meant they were supposed to be able to administer their own medications to and for them selves. Occasionally we had a treatment or two to do. We had clinic hours once a week at which time we did blood pressures and minor interventions as needed. These residents did not require the same amount of care so this level of care was not as heavily regulated as Long-Term Care.

One day I was in the dining room distributing medications to those who were ready to take them when one of the residents called me over to her. I leaned in real close to see what she had to say. She said, "It is so refreshing that you take the time to speak to us and greet us in the morning when you are giving medications". She said something about my smile. It brightened up her day.

This comment both touched and broke my heart. It was textbook knowledge that we as professionals are supposed to engage our residents, not just hand them their medications. Not only is it text book, it is common courtesy. I knew that common courtesy was a concept from the past. I thanked her for sharing her feelings with me and told her she also brightened up my day by noticing that quality in me. I was glad that someone appreciated my kindness and efficiency.

All was well in the clinic but Steve was having trouble in the Long-Term Care Unit. He'd hired a new DSD/MDS coordinator and things were not working out. When things totally fell apart he asked if I would transfer to the health care unit and be the DSD/ MDS coordinator. The unit only had twenty- eight beds. I asked myself how hard could that job be? I told him yes.

At the time Steve blamed all the problems concerning this department on the former employee's lack of experience etc. etc. But it didn't take long for me to see that was not solely the case.

This facility had been in existence for many years now but they had no DSD materials. There were no orientation manuals or records of staff training. They had no records of Licenses or CPR status that I could find. The MDS's were behind but they were planning to install a new computer system supposedly to make things better. The office was a mess. I told Steve I had not done MDS's in a while so I would like to have some refresher training. I never got it.

To make a long story short, I established each of these departmental areas from the ground up. I organized and updated my self to do the MDS's and in a few months began to get things on tract. In addition to completing the MDS's I was responsible for scheduling and conducting care conferences with the residents and responsible parties who could attend them. I did it all in stride. I began to receive compliments from staff, residents and family about the difference I was making in the facility.

During one Care Conference a family person addressed Steve and his boss Lori saying, you guys must be glad to have her here. No one ever took the time to review my dads' status with me like this before.

My research was always thorough. I always did a personal assessment of each resident as well as interview staff members involved with that resident and reviewed the chart before conferences. This was also how I compiled the data I needed to complete the MDS.

Neither Steve nor Lori seemed to be happy to hear this compliment although Lori had once told me herself that she'd never known anyone in the business as knowledgeable as I was. This family person had no problem expressing her self when things were going bad. For her to give this type of compliment meant she was really impressed with my service but not to impressed with the service she'd received up until then.

Lori was the Administrator. She appeared to be young. She was Santa Barbara style beautiful. This means she was blonde, thin but shapely and vain. She had style. She was articulate and involved in all the happenings at Vista. Because she was so involved I believe she took this comment as a personal insult. This I knew could be a blessing and a curse. In spite of this, I was not a person to sit back and complain about problems. I was more of a problem solver. I still wanted to fix problems.

I found that most of the problems were directly related to systems failure. This included lack of systems implementation or lack of oversight concerning use of systems, in short poor leadership. I felt that low morale, substandard work performance and poor reviews were all a function of poor management. This was simple to me. That was why I worked so hard to build teamwork, accountability and reliability in any capacity I was assigned to work in. The problem to me was that most managers I knew were not willing to implement and master these three key elements as part of their professional skills training.

I did not and still don't like confrontation but know it is vital that a manager be able to confront issues when they arise. I do not even "enjoy" holding people accountable. It is much easier to overlook poor work performance that is until it affects a resident, generates a complaint or causes tension between staff members and shifts. Then the problem still has to be dealt with. I was less frustrated and happier when I was solving problems not stewing in them.

With change comes pain. That was becoming my motto. It wasn't long before certain staff members began to give me a hard time. I forgot to mention for the record I was one of three Blacks who worked on this whole campus. In the Health Center there were two of us.

Gala the other Black person was a Unit Clerk. I thought we were cool until the party got started. I don't mean a fun party either. I'm saying I thought we were cool until stuff got stirred up.

You know the scenario by now. When I asked questions I got smart answers like "I don't see why that's any of your business"! Excuse me! I am a part of this team. "So what, I don't answer to you!" That was from a floor nurse who later was found to have a drug problem and was stealing narcotics from patients. The weapon of sabotage, "withholding information" was implemented right away. Asking me to do things to overload me or manipulate me like "I have an admission coming in. Will you help me? But the person I'm supposed to be helping leaves all the work to me. I help with answering phones so they stopped answering the phones all together. The whole time they are engaged in this behavior no one is offering or qualified to help me get my work done. My boss could not do my job because he was not qualified or knowledgeable enough to do it even though he was the Director. When I needed help I had to call the corporate consultant or figure it out myself.

I asked myself, how do I keep getting into this position? The majority of the time the people that were over me could not even do the work they were asking me to do. If you ask me this is a major problem in the work place.

Over and over I had to prove myself. When I did, the person over me, or those around me, felt threatened. Yet they say there is a nursing shortage.

I want to scream at those that say there is a nursing shortage and say **Hey!**

If you need nurses act like it! I want to scream at the self-centered insecure people that cause so much trouble for people like my self. **Hey! I'm not here to take your job! I'm trying to do mine! If you feel threatened because I do well then you should do better! Stop cheating your employer, yourself and your patients!** The sad thing is that many of the ones who gave me such a hard time are the very ones who sit back and complain about their bosses and co-workers. Even when I didn't like my place of work I always put my best foot forward. I always gave 110% of what I knew how to give.

There are many people that don't have jobs and many places were there are no jobs available. Be thankful to God that you have a job! Show that you are thankful by doing a good job and God will bless the work of your hands.

When I got to the place where I was complaining and hating to go to work that meant I'd done everything possible to try to improve the working conditions of my environment.

That also meant it was time for me to go! I was not going to let any job suck the life out of me or strip me of my identity!

So many people don't know who they are so they have a need to fit in. They are too weak to stand-alone. I was always polite to my co-workers and subordinates even when I corrected them. I participated in potlucks and parties as I could but did not let job related events interfere with my personal life.

Being a nurse was not my whole life it was one of the many gifts and talents that I chose to share with others. I've heard of and known good nursing students and nurses who quit training or working because the work was so demanding, some of them quit right after graduating from nursing school.

The truth of the matter is that nursing is hard work if you do it well. There is little reward in it. It is not glamorous at all. It is a career for one who has a servant's heart. If you do not have a servant's heart you should not be in the medical profession at all! Not as a manager or in any other capacity. If you are, you are the reason there is a nursing shortage! I say this because servant hood is not about profit or gain. It is about giving. It is about meeting the needs of others.

I could have stayed in the clinic but I couldn't choose the path of least resistance. Steve asked for my help so I gave my help.

It didn't take long before my relationship with Steve deteriorated. Because of my efficiency I was constantly asked to do more. I felt like this. Don't keep adding to my plate just because I can do it. Learn from my example. If I can do it so can you/ they. If you/ they can't do what I can do, then appreciate me for what I bring to the table. Show me you appreciate me by compensating me well. Compensation for me is not just monetary. Treat me with respect! I don't need to be you. You don't need to be me. As long as we respect each other's strengths and weakness we can function as a team. I now know that part of the reason for that decline came from me listening to Albertah's advice.

In spite of the things I'd heard and in spite of my husbands advice I kept an open mind concerning her. I even had her come and provide an in-service to the staff about Alzheimer's. She actually did a great presentation. I was proud to have her as a guest speaker. We kept in touch. When we talked I told her of the problems I was now facing at the Monte. She advised me to politely distance my self from Steve. Don't let them get over on you. You're doing his job. If he wants you to do his work tell them you want a raise in pay, that kind of advice. I agreed with everything she told me but I might have lasted longer or even been able to stay in the middle of the road in that setting if I hadn't taken her advice. You live and you learn though. Now I know it was not meant for me to stay in the middle of the road. So I made the right choice in the long run.

I began to realize this group did not want things to get better. They were backbiters, back stabbers, whiners and complainers. Like others I'd dealt with they did not know how to fix the problems themselves but they also did not want anyone else to fix them. They say misery loves company. It does.

This particular morning Steve was in his office. I was in mine. Yes I had an office this time. I was working on MDS's. I needed some information about a resident from the RNA, a Hispanic aide. So I approached her and asked her my question. "If you want to know, go look for your self." That was the response I got. She was a subordinate. I was a manager. That was the straw that broke the camels back! I called her into my office. I looked her in the face. "The next time I ask you a question, I expect an answer. Not a smart one but an answer". She began to explain. "I just meant if you need to know you should go check for yourself". I explained, "I did check for myself. I did my own assessment. I just wanted your professional input because the section of the MDS I'm working on is about the work you did with this resident. The information they require is cumulative. My assessment just tells how they are doing at the time of my assessment". She could see I was upset. I went on to say from now on you will treat me with the same respect I give you. Is that clear? A bit shaken up she said yes, it is clear. Next I marched into Steve's office and let him know I was tired of the way the staff was treating me and I wanted him to do something about it! What? He asked? Call the ones who've been giving me a hard time into your office right now! I will set them straight! I just need you to back me up! He said ok.

There were three key staff members who were making my life miserable. It only takes a few you know. They are often the ring leaders, the ones who have the clout. In every situation I'd dealt with up to this point it was clear that these kind could and did influence everyone else's behavior. If I knew then what I know now I would have found out who they were in the beginning, started a paper trail on them and fired them off the top. Oh I forgot I tried that before. I just didn't have the backing I needed at the time.

I called them into Steve's office. I was so angry I was shaking inside. The office was small so we were in tight quarters. I made it clear that things were going to be different from here on out! I was through being polite and patient! You have disrespected me for the last time! You have pushed me and pushed me. Obviously you wanted to see if I could go here. So now we are here! With my hands on my hips, feet pacing the floor and finger pointed in a face. The one I pointed to was a nurse. She snarled. Don't put your finger in my face!

Steve tried to explain to me how she felt. "It is a cultural thing". He stated. He was White. She was Hispanic. This infuriated me. Nearly exploding I said, "I am sick and tired of hearing about this cultural thing! If any one has the right to talk about cultural differences it is me! I am the only Black person in here besides Gala and she's a part of their mess. If anything, they need to understand my culture. I'm the minority here! We are expressive people. We communicate with our hands and body language. When we are upset we are very expressive and I am upset! I further explained. I've done each and every one of your jobs before! I've taught people how to do your jobs. I am not a novice. I know more about what you are supposed to be doing than you do, so you better start showing me some respect! I went on and on until I felt satisfied we had an understanding. To my surprise Steve backed me up. We finished our meeting and that was that.

Things immediately improved between them and me after that. I wish I could say that things improved overall. The improvement was temporary.

Remember earlier I told you nursing homes got surveyed annually. Well the time for our survey was approaching so the corporate nurse started coming to our facility to help prepare us for survey. She was cool. I appreciated her input and her support. She immediately picked up on many of the things that were wrong in our facility. She asked me what is going on here. I told her what was wrong from my perspective and all that I'd done to correct the problems since I'd been there. She voiced her frustrations to me. I confirmed her frustrations and voiced mine to her. One of them was the fact that Steve had no regard or concern for the state regulations. Many of the things she told him we needed to do to stay out of trouble I had also told him and Lori. The problem was they didn't listen. He'd told me he didn't care for DHS and he felt they were unreasonable in their expectations. I agreed with some of his opinions but tried to convince him we still needed to comply with the regulations. Now we were going to see were we stood.

When the surveyors come to survey a facility they come with one of the latest reports they received from the MDS database. The MDS calculates and triggers problem areas in a facility concerning resident care. The good thing about this is the facility can use this information as a quality assurance tool. They can intervene and correct any possible problems or problematic areas before the surveyors come. It was my job to generate this report and give it to Steve. I can assure you I did my job.

Survey time is always stressful. When this time came it was no different. It was actually one of the worst surveys I'd participated in. Steve was the DON. He'd been there longer than me but he kept disappearing when the surveyors or staff, me included needed him to answer questions. So the surveyor and Lori began to rely on me for more and more information. Over and over they came to me. I was as professional, helpful and as truthful as I could be until I began to hear reports that Steve was belligerent and argumentative with the surveyors. They became frustrated with him. They reported that he was not spending enough time in the facility to properly oversee its functions. To that accusation he reportedly demanded that they prove it! Here I was trying to manage the survey. He was intentionally inflaming their frustrations. After a few days, I told Lori I was not answering any more questions for Steve. She then assumed the responsibility for his problems and the facility problems. I continued to assist her best I could. At the end of one horrible day the surveyors announced they would be extending the survey because of what they were finding. They did.

When it ended we got ten citations or deficiencies. I don't recall the exact category. The majority of them were directly related to management issues, lack of systems, lack of over site of systems and things like that. Surveys are a matter of public record so I don't mind sharing this information. It was good they were not the severe kind but I was very frustrated that we got the ones we got because they all could have been avoided.

The corporate nurse, I can't recall her name, was not too happy either. Part of her job was to help us do our plan of corrections. After talking with Steve about this it was becoming painfully clear that they wanted me to take the rap for the facility problems. I remembered how he said to me your assessments are more accurate than the nurses and you don't even work the floor! I knew the MDS assessment played a direct role in the surveyors focus. The consultant told me she explained when they asked why this had not happened before. The MDS's probably were not being done accurately before. Now they are!

To pay me back for doing such a good job, Steve gave me the assignment of doing the plan of corrections. Around this time he also offered to make me his Assistant DON in addition to my other responsibilities. I was already filling two positions and it took all of my time to build these areas up to the level they were now functioning at. I was finally caught up with the MDS's. The tension had mounted between Steve and me to the point that he now wanted me to train one of the clinic nurses to help me with the MDS's. This sounded good but I knew he was worried I was going to quit or he was going to try and get rid of me. So this time I taught her the basics. I did not teach her everything I knew. I was not going to fully equip my replacement. I'd been down that road before. I declined the added responsibilities of being the ADON and the raise that was supposed to come with it.

Because my load was so heavy, I did the plan of corrections at home in my off time and submitted a request for payment for the extra work I'd done. I was not salaried. I was getting paid an hourly wage so I thought this was fair. Steve and Lori did not like this. They made it clear they would pay me this time but don't expect it in the future!

Steve and I were communicating mostly by email now even though our offices were right down the hall from each other. I lost all respect for Steve by this point. Lori was going to stick by his side no matter what. They were white you know. I knew there was no way I would have kept my job if I were in his shoes. I'd been fired for much less than this. I knew it was time for me to leave. On my next day off I went to work, packed my things and quit.

I was told Steve only lasted several more months after I quit. I was also told the facility came under investigation for some resident care issues that occurred during the time I was there. One of the residents fell and broke her hip. She did not receive the proper follow up care. This was one of the things I'd voiced concerns about to Steve. I never learned the outcome of that investigation.

Chapter 15

Maybe I just needed to work as a floor nurse. Maybe I was just not cut out for management. Being in management meant, having no integrity. At this point I just wanted a job I could do without hating it. I just wanted to be able to pay my bills.

I called my old boss Sherie in Santa Maria to see if they needed any nurses. She said she would gladly take me back.

Several of the employees and residents that were there the first time I worked there were still there. It felt like going home. In spite of the frustrations I had before it felt good to be back.

The Villa had new owners and was under new management. Lori and Connie were gone. I had hopes that things would at the least be tolerable. I just wanted to do my work and go home at the end of the day.

It was hard work before. It was ridiculously hard work now. The paper work was endless. One occurrence such as a skin tear or the discovery of a new pressure ulcer generated a minimum of ten steps to be completed. That meant you had to stop doing what ever you were doing. Gather your treatment supplies, usually found in the Treatment Cart. Go and assess the problem. Take pictures of the problem to properly identify it. Label the photos. Treat the problem. At some point before your shift ended, submit a request for the treatment you did to the MD to cover your butt. Technically we were not supposed to do a treatment without a Doctor's order. Care Plan the problem. Complete an incident report (two pages long) this included investigating how the skin tear occurred, what could have contributed to it and what could have been done to prevent it. Document it in the nurse's notes.

Notify the dietary department, the responsible party, the DON, write it on the communication sheet and pass it on in report.

Do you have any idea how easy it is for an elderly person to sustain a skin tear? Can you imagine how much work is involved to prevent skin problems? The occurrence of a skin tear alone could take up at least an hour of your time just to complete the paper work. We were required to do this with each skin tear. If there were two, double the time it would take to complete the paper work.

Now remember we had a minimum of 28-30 residents, meds to give within certain time frames and routine charting to do. If I had a resident sustain a skin tear, one fall or one be impacted during my shift I could just expect every thing else to back up on me. If my CNAs were busy or if I simply had a sorry CNA assigned to my team that day it would be Hell, literal torment. Often I did not get help. I rarely asked for it because I knew there was none to get. When I did ask it was because I was desperate and still did not get any help.

I remember vividly one day asking the ADON Ellen for help several times. I was drowning. My residents were complaining about the care or should I say lack of care they were getting from their CNA. It was almost noon. Several of them were still in bed and had not been attended to since breakfast. Each time I approached the CNA about it she was unconcerned. She took long breaks and took her time doing everything she did that day. Ellen did not help me. No one helped me. When I finally did go to lunch late that afternoon I was so overwhelmed I spent my thirty-minute lunch break in tears. I hated to see any patient/resident being neglected. Later that afternoon I saw both the DON and the ADON in the office laughing and talking. Ellen always made sure she had several long smoke breaks each day as well as a lunch break. This day was no different. My shift was supposed to end at three-thirty. Around five PM Sherie saw that I was still working and asked why are you still here? This was nothing new. It was routine to work this way. I wanted to ask, why do you have to ask? Instead I told her what a horrible day I had, what a horrible CNA I had assigned to my team and how Ellen did not help me at all when I asked her to at least deal with the CNA. She acknowledged my feelings of frustration and said she was trying to get good help for us.

I put in a lot of over time. That was the only way I could do the job right.

The biggest frustration for me while I was there this time was that I was supposed to be a floor nurse. I had my own team I was responsible for. I was frequently asked to go and help other nurses do things like start IV's because Ellen the ADON could not start IV's. No one covered my team while I was gone no matter how long it took me. I did not want extra responsibilities like these. I went back to the floor to avoid this.

As an ADON I was required to help my staff with IV's, admissions and everything. Ellen was the ADON. She should be able to provide this kind of support. Why the double standard? Why was I always expected to do more when others could get away with doing less? Even some of the Philippine staff had this figured out.

Because of my experience I was asked to be the house supervisor at times. When I was I was everywhere. You name it I did it. It was my job to support the nursing staff how ever I could. I knew what it was like to work the floor. It was horrible! I tried to handle the admissions when they came so the floor nurse would not have to.

One particular day we had several admissions scheduled to arrive. Although they were scheduled several hours apart I was still tied up when the second one was coming in the building. I called Dora a Philippine nurse who had just arrived to work the evening shift to tell her she would need to do the admission that was coming to her floor. She belligerently asked, why can't you do it? I explained we had two admissions. I was still working on one. This resident had multiple pressure ulcers, around seven or eight and the paperwork was enormous. She went on to let me know that was my problem and my job! I in turn let her know that I knew what my job was. I also knew what hers was. My shift was ending. Hers was beginning. So she would need to take over where I had to leave off!

I later reported to Sherie the severity of that resident's condition. I had not seen any one neglected this bad in years. It brought tears to my eyes. According to the new abuse reporting laws her condition needed to be reported to the proper authorities. Sherrie did not agree but after some persuasion changed her mind. The resident was in severe pain from her sores. We placed her on Morphine to try and make her comfortable. She only survived about a week after that. When she died I was not at work but during that night I dreamt about her. I could hear her talking to me in my sleep. I don't remember what she said. The next day when I went to work I learned she died during the night. When her family member came to retrieve her belongings he confirmed the time of her death to be around the same time I was dreaming about her.

It was a good thing that we reported this patient's condition because later a State person came to investigate the situation and agreed she had been neglected. The facility she came from was given a deficiency. If we had not reported the situation we would have had to prove that her condition did not come about while she was in our care. The surveyor complimented me for my very thorough documentation and acknowledged it must have taken me a long time to do this.

I later learned that Dora was reprimanded for her smart mouth. The professional term is – insubordination. But that did not change the behaviors. So they would not have to deal with the conflicts between the PM shift nurses and the day shift staff the DON tried to have an extra person come in and help with the admissions. Go figure! Why didn't they have to work overtime if needed? Why did they get catered to? One could say it was because most of them already worked two jobs. Then I would have to ask the question. Is that fair to the rest of the staff that because they have another job they should not have to do a good job here? This was one of the primary reasons I didn't like to work double shifts. After eight hours I knew I was no longer as alert and sharp as I should be. I didn't want to make mistakes. I knew that I would be held accountable for my mistakes even if I'd worked a double shift to help the facility out with their staffing needs.

It was routine that the evening shift nurses, primarily certain Philippine ones came to work and expected everything to be done before they got there. They expected to come in, do their weekly summaries and then pass medications without interruptions. Often I saw them come in, gather at the desk, socialize, pass around pictures etc. etc. The PM CNAs were sitting down for lunch in groups before the day shift could even leave the building! They would pretend not to know or refuse to know the answers to questions in order to keep from being interrupted by families while doing their work. The few times I worked the evening shift I was busy the whole time just like when I worked the day shift. I could not escape the double standard. Because I had a conscience I would not leave the work for the next shift nurse to do unless I absolutely had to but when I needed help and was bogged down I could not get help. Was that because I was competent and they felt I could handle things on my own? Was it because I was Black? It was very difficult to determine why this was. My competence never got me promoted only used!

Even the Philippine nurses who were foreigners were treated with more respect than I was as an American born, Military Brat, and Minister of the Gospel who happened to be a Black Nurse.

For years now certain hospitals had programs in place to recruit nurses from the

Philippines. I've yet to see any such program created to recruit Black nurses from Africa or other cities or states in the U.S. to come to California.

I was a perfectly qualified Black nurse who was consistently treated like a third class citizen and I was supposed to like it.

The second biggest frustration for me while working there this time around was seeing how management catered to Ms Jackie. I forgot to mention Jackie in my first Villa experience. Jackie was a very knowledgeable, very experienced older white nurse with a rough exterior. She was an LVN who had been there for many years. The first time I worked at the Villa Jackie gave me a hard time. She was the kind of person who tested you to see what you were made of. She knew the answer to most any question one might ask but she wanted to see if I knew what she knew. If I didn't, shame on me. She would openly complain or talk about me to other staff. It was common knowledge that Jackie was hard to work under or with at times because of her disposition. She sent nurses home in tears just because she could and she was allowed to get away with it. She even told the resident's off when she felt like it. One of her resident's often came to me to ask for his pain medication because he said Jackie was mean to him when he asked her for it. In spite of her ways I liked Jackie. I realized it was just her way. It was just her personality. But I did feel her behavior should not have been tolerated. It bordered on being abusive. It was unfair to the rest of the staff myself included. And it certainly was not good for employee or resident morale.

Now that I'd experienced the things I'd experienced I really had a problem with this. Over the past five years I had to be overly diplomatic and tactful in my approach when dealing with staff members on any level. If I was frustrated I was not supposed to show my frustrations. As a supervisor I was not supposed to supervise yet I was supposed to supervise. I had great responsibilities with little authority or backing. I had to be all to all, but people like Jackie could treat people the way they wanted to and get away with it.

Exactly what was it about me that caused such a stir? I sought an answer to this for many years. The few times I had occasion to talk with other Black nurses about this issue. They voiced similar if not identical opinions and experiences to me.

One year I traveled to Washington DC on family business. A relative of mine was recovering from a severe illness. He was readmitted to Washington Hospital Center for follow up care. Everywhere we went in the city we saw Black people. Therefore everywhere we went in the hospital we saw Black people. There were Black CNAs, Black Nurses (LVNs and RN's), Black Doctors and Housekeepers. There were Black Cashiers in the cafeteria. I even saw a Black Anesthesiologist. I couldn't believe my eyes. I asked one of the nurses. What type of nurse are you, LVN or RN? She told me she was an RN. Forgive me for being nosey I added. I am just amazed at the number of Black staff I see here! I've never seen this before. Where are you from? She asked. California. I replied. She confirmed that she heard it was that way in California and many other places. What I was seeing there was a rare occurrence in other parts of the Country. Some of the staff was helpful and polite. Others were not. Some had attitudes. Others did not. I saw this with the White staff as well as with the Blacks.

I later talked with a nurse from the DC area about the obstacles I faced repeatedly during my career. She told me, "We don't put up with that mess out here! It doesn't matter who you are if you get out of line we deal with you and we don't have to wait for management to do it either". "If you came here with the skills and experience you have you would be respected for who you are and what you bring to the table". She was an LVN.

My mind went back to the time when Albertah and I worked together at the Gardens. It was obvious that Janice and Robin were very nervous about the two of us being there together. If we were in a room together, it didn't matter if it was my office or Alberta's office. Janice would make it a point to walk by and check on us. I could feel the distrust and suspicion they had concerning us. It was annoying. It reminded me of the way some store clerks watch and act like they think we, us Black folks might steal something when we are in the store. It amazed me that we were always out numbered but our superiors still felt threatened by our presence. So, I thought. There is strength in numbers.

During my time at the Villa, I was one of two Black nurses. I had several conversations with the other Black nurse about the injustices I saw while working there. I knew her from the first time I'd worked there. She had many things to say to me about the differences in the culture here in America and her culture. She was from Belize. She asked me not to mention her in this book so I won't repeat her observations. I will say that I noticed how she changed over the years. When she first came to Santa Maria she was new to the United States. She was very polite and soft spoken. She answered yes maam and no maam when she was addressed. . Now she cursed when addressed, appeared to be frustrated most of the time and seemed hard like she developed a "thick skin". Based on the accounts she gave me I attributed this change to living in America and having to deal with the racism that is still so prevalent here.

There were mumblings going around about Sherie taking a medical leave. I knew this meant she would probably be retiring soon. The word was that Ellen did not want to be DON. She had other interest that conflicted with her taking the position. Being on my feet for long hours was taking a toll on me. I wasn't getting any younger. My legs began to respond to the constant pounding. Knowing and dreading the responsibilities that came with being a DON I really didn't want to go there again but my body was telling me "look here, I can't take working the floor any more" so I went to the administrator, Paul to offer my assistance. I gave him my employment history package, complete with a resume and told him I was available to help in a supervisory capacity if needed. If any changes were going to be made in management, please keep me in mind. He thanked me for my willingness to help and my inquiry but relayed that he did not fore see any changes being made. Shortly after this changes were made. Ellen assigned Ginny to be the supervisor.

Ginny was an LVN. Of course she was White. She'd been there several years. She was cool and all but I did not like her work ethic. She often left things undone. Sherie and Ellen both had complained to me on other occasions about Ginny's work. They talked about moving her to another team because she could not handle the load on station three. Now all of the sudden they wanted her to supervise others. Here we go again. The double standard was in effect. There were several times Sherrie chewed me out for not doing a care plan correctly or as she put it, behaving unprofessionally. But Ginny could half do her work over and over and be given supervisor responsibilities.

This was too much for me. When I thought about how the Philippine nurses were treated, how Jackie was treated, how Vera was treated, how Ginny was treated and how I was treated, I had to accept the reality that they all had priority over me.

I must tell you about Vera so you will fully understand my train of thought. Vera was an LVN. She also was White. When I met Vera she seemed cool. She invited me to lunch and schooled me about the working environment. Her disposition changed towards me when she learned that I'd been there before and I was pretty savvy about things already.

A few times she tried to instruct me to do things contrary to my experience and work standards. I politely acknowledged her input but continued to do what I knew to do. She let me know then that Jackie told her to do things this way and Jackie would deal with me like she'd dealt with her. She'd sent her home crying several times in the past. When she saw that I was very capable of dealing with Jackie she became my enemy.

At first I thought I was tripping. I would leave instructions for the next shift nurse. They'd disappear. I started being extra careful not to forget things. Then it became more apparent that I wasn't tripping. It was Vera trying to sabotage me. One day I stayed late to make sure I did everything I had to do to complete a new order for one of my patients. I put it on the communication board, the calendar at the nurse's station, the MAR, told the patient and charted what I'd done. I covered all the bases. Vera was assigned to work that station the next day. I was at station one but I could hear her all the way down the hall yelling and arguing with a patient/resident. "You have an appointment today! She yelled! He was telling her he did not have an appointment. I was disturbed that she would talk to a resident in the tone of voice she was using but I did not interfere. A few minutes later she called me from her station phone and accused me of making a mistake about the appointment. I informed her that I did not make a mistake. The patient was correct. He did not have an appointment that day. All the information was available to her in all the appropriate places. She just needed to go back and verify it. Again she called me up and continued to insist I'd made a mistake. I followed her to her Med cart and showed her the information was written on the MAR. There it was right in plain site. By this point I was frustrated with her and asked her what was her problem. She apologized when I didn't back down. Now I began to think she was seriously strange like she had a split personality or something.

I reported my concern to Sherrie along with the fact that I was hearing rumors that Vera was out to get me. She'd told people to watch out for me because I was out to get them but also told other people she couldn't stand me and was going to get me fired. Sherrie did not offer much support except to say that Vera reported to her that others had treated her that way when she first came to the Villa. Maybe she was just treating me the way she'd been treated.

I'd heard some serious accusation about Vera's function ability but chose to keep an open mind about the accusations. Now I began to believe the rumors. Vera continued to play her games. I continued to complain about the situation to no avail. Then one day Ellen told me I was assigned to work station two the next day. She made it clear Vera was to have station three instead of station two, her favorite station. She told me Vera was not going to like it but that was the way it was to be.

I accepted her instructions. The next day when Vera came to work she like Ellen said, had a fit about her assignment. "I'm not working that station! Station two is my station! I calmly told her Ellen made the assignment not me. She continued to loud talk me at the station. There were staff and residents nearby, "I don't care who made it. I'm not working it! I continued to prepare for my day and told her she or I could talk to Sherrie about it when she gets here, something like that. She continued to yell. "You can do what you want to do! I'm not working it! I'm going to call Paul!" Now she was getting on, correction had gotten on my last nerve. I firmly told her I don't care who you call! You are no different then any one else around here! I did what I was told to do! So do what you are told to do! She grabbed the employee phone directory and stormed off. I proceeded to do my work.

When Sherrie arrived I relayed to her that we had a problem. To my surprise she let me know how disappointed she was with "our" lack of professionalism. Our, included me. Baffled I asked what she meant. She dismissed me with a wave of her hand. I will deal with you later. She said. I was baffled and hurt. Apparently Vera called her instead of Paul. Sherrie knew me well. We went way back. She also knew of Vera's reputation. There had been multiple complaints against her from staff as well as patients. But she chose to listen to Vera. I realized at that point I'd been set up again. I went to Ellen and told her what happened. She offered no explanation for Sherrie's behavior. Nor did she offer to fix the problem she created after all; she should have let Vera know her assignment was changed. She just confirmed that they expected Vera to act the way she acted. I was wounded. I couldn't sleep that night. I reviewed the event in my mind over and over. I decided to make a written complaint about it. At the end of my account of the event I stated that I would apologize to Vera if Sherrie wanted me to but only out of respect for her authority. I also stated I would not let Vera harass me any more. I never got a response from Sherrie to my complaint. I later heard that Sherrie did conduct an investigation. Ellen told me not to worry Vera would eventually be her own demise.

From that point on I wrote down the things Vera did to me. I made copies of her nurse's notes, which she used to implicate me of things. After more complaints from other staff and residents Vera was finally no longer an employee of the Villa.

My point, it took all of that to get Vera off my back. The Philippine nurses were running things. Ginny was now supervising. Where did that leave me?

I learned from Alberta of a new job opportunity. She told me it was a good job. She said there were some minor issues but overall things were good there. Because of my distrust concerning this person, I knew her history. I asked if she'd mind working together again. We had a complicated relationship. She of course told me not at all. The benefit to me was better pay, thirty an hour instead of twenty-five. It was a specialty I'd never done before.

I applied and got the new job so after about a year of trying to make it work I quit the Villa for the second time. When Jackie learned I was leaving again she came to me in tears and let me know she would miss me. I was totally surprised!

Chapter 16

Once again I was excited and looking forward to something new. When I interviewed at the new place, I was surprised to learn that the manager was an old classmate of mine from Santa Barbara City College. Her name was Marie. She was young, small in stature and Philippine. Her speech was broken, her affect flat but I dismissed my initial feelings about my first encounter with her. I was used to it. I did notice her lack of femininity and her attire was that of a man. After our interview she told me Norma would need to interview me too. I went back for a second interview. Norma was also Philippine. Her affect was even flatter then Marie's. I could not read her expressions. She was well dressed. She appeared to be more feminine than Marie. I noticed uncomfortably how closely they worked together. I later named them the Asian Persuasion. Roberta had warned me about their relationship but also down played its relevance. I had the sense that they would stick together through thick or thin. This concerned me but I believed it shouldn't matter. I would simply do my job and go home at the end of the day. After they reviewed my resume I asked some questions. I'd heard things about the center even before Roberta mentioned it to me. They were not good things. They couldn't keep staff. I asked why other nurses had left. What would be expected of me, things like that? I made it clear that I was interested in the position but nervous because I'd never done this type of work before. After some reassurance and an agreement to pay me what I asked for, I was hired. The one stipulation was that I would not get my increase until I passed my orientation period of two months. Under the circumstances I thought this was fair. Out with the old, on to the new, I was going to be a Dialysis nurse.

When I was in school the thought of doing dialysis petrified me. It was so detailed and required so much responsibility. I realized that I'd grown considerably to even consider doing it now. Like many other areas in nursing Dialysis had changed a great deal too.

About a week before I was to start orientation for my new job I had this dream.

3/29/04

Me at work

Looked like, felt like the Villa but I could not see well.

It was as though my sight was veiled.

I could see things when I looked down but not when I looked up.

Albertah came to me in the hallway. I said hello. I was glad to know she was there.

She was reserved and distant. I wanted to hug her but didn't. She began to tell me things to do. She asked me did I have my face /head shield on. I told her I did not but began to cry because I could not see. She did not seem to be concerned. I asked her were do I get the shield from? Before I could go into the utility room to look for it she warned me that the lady in charge was coming toward me. The lady came and asked me about my shield. I told her I'd been instructed about it but hadn't had the chance to get it yet. I didn't know where to get it from. Started to explain the need for it to me but seemed to be understanding. (I got the feeling that Albertah was trying to make me nervous).

I remember waking up disturbed. As you already know I did not fully trust Albertah. I knew if she was in my dream this could not be good. I knew that someone from my past was going to cause me anguish again. I prayed. Oh Lord not again! But I felt peace in my spirit that it would not be the same as before so I reported to work for orientation when I was supposed to.

From the out side the center did not even look like a medical facility. When you entered the building you were in the lobby and receptionist area. Behind the receptionist area were rooms for chart storage, peritoneal dialysis education, instruction and exam rooms for out patient services. Then you came to the Dieticians office, the Dr'sCrones office, he was the Medical Director and then Marie's office.

Immediately past Marie's office was the Dialysis Unit. The unit was a rectangular room. On one end was the Nurse's Station. It was a small area equipped with a desk, phone access, cabinets and a refrigerator for storage. Our unit was small. Each station consisted of a reclining chair and a dialysis machine. Most of our supplies were kept in the center of the room.

We provided treatments to our patients in two shifts. The first shift started at seven AM. The next shift started after the first shift treatments were complete. A treatment began with an assessment which included taking vital signs, listening to breath sounds, checking for edema and evaluating each patients overall condition. Then the patient is connected to a Dialysis machine.

The connection is made by accessing a vascular site that has already been put in place. There are three types of vascular devices. The permanent catheters are placed in the upper outer chest wall. They have dual ports, extensions that protrude from the chest wall. When accessing the permacath it is first aspirated, suctioned to remove the Heparin that was placed in it to keep it patent. Next it is flushed with Normal Saline. The venous port is again primed with Heparin. Then both ports are connected to the extension tubing that is set up on the machine. Fistulas and Grafts are peripheral sites usually located in the arms. When accessing a Fistula or Graft the skin is palpated to find the site. In some cases the site is anesthetized in others it is not. Special needles equipped with tubing are then inserted into the vascular devise. The venous port is primed with Heparin. Both tubes are then connected to the extension tubing set up on the machine.

On the machine side of things, each machine is cleaned after each treatment, internally and externally. They are tested each day before the shift begins and programmed to give the proper treatment as prescribed. Bags of Normal Saline and Heparin are connected to the extension tubing. The tubing is threaded thru the machine and connected to the patient just before the treatment begins.

On average, each treatment last from two to three and one half hours. During the treatment all the patients' blood is sucked out of their blood stream, cleansed, dialyzed and returned to them via the tubing. Normally the kidneys perform this task. They filter waste products and toxins out of the blood stream but when they fail this must be done artificially. Patients are monitored very closely for complications. Complications include sudden changes in blood pressure, fainting, chest pain, acute infection also known as sepsis, nausea, vomiting, cramps, thrombosis and formation of blood clots just to name a few. If interventions are not implemented immediately when complications occur death may occur.

There are two types of Dialysis. Hemodialysis is done by accessing the blood stream via a vascular device. Peritoneal Dialysis is done by accessing the peritoneal cavity thru a catheter in the abdomen. I was involved with Hemodialysis.

It was not hard for me to see how vicious and cruel this disease was. In addition to Kidney Failure many of our patients had other major diseases like Diabetes, Hypertension and Cardiac disease to further compound their health problems. I gained an immediate respect for anyone who had the courage to live with Kidney Failure. Although necessary, the treatment protocol is extremely confining. After treatment most patients are very weak and hungry. Can you imagine having your blood sucked out of you two or three days a week for several hours a day?

The first day of orientation I was glad to see a familiar face. I was looking forward to working with someone I knew. I knew we had some differences but felt we were both mature enough to work through them. When I saw Roberta I wanted to hug her but her body language told me not to. She acted like she didn't know me. I was puzzled and disturbed by this. We'd shared meals at each other's homes! What was this all about? Roberta called me later that evening to see how my day went. She explained that she was not ignoring me to be mean. She was playing the game. If they think we really know each other or get along too well they will start tripping with us, she said. I knew this to be a true assessment but did not feel we had to hide who we were to the extent that we ignored each other at work. Naturally I talked with my husband about the situation. He told me not to trust her just like he had told me not to trust Albertah. At some point after the discussion with my husband I remembered my dream. This was the way Albertah had behaved in my dream. I made a mental note of this and braced myself for what ever was next. Characters in dreams are not always exact but I knew this was symbolic.

Each day two nurses were scheduled to work the floor. One was to act as a supervisor in addition to working the floor. Several techs were assigned to assist with patient care. They could not do assessments or connect patients with permacaths so they put the patients on who had fistulas and grafts. In addition to this the techs had other special duties.

The staff was a mixed group. We had two White nurses at the time, Lucy and Lori, one Philippine nurse, Delia, two Black nurses, Roberta and me. The same is true of the techs. We had two White techs, three Hispanics and three Philippine techs. Now the Philippine staff was in charge.

My training began with following the techs. It progressed to following Marie. She was very particular about making sure the new nurses learned the ropes from her. Things were going well working with Marie. I felt she was very fast and competent. She assured me I was doing well so I absorbed everything I could as she trained me. After she expressed her comfort with what I knew she turned me over to work with Roberta. We worked with the permacath patients. When seven o- clock came we opened the doors. The patients came in in no particular order. I was instructed to start with whoever came in first. Because I was extra, things went pretty smooth. After we got every patient hooked up and their treatments started we had to draw up medications. One nurse would draw up the meds and give them. The other nurse was to change the dressing around the permacath. This was done to prevent infections at the site. Roberta had not been with the company for very long so she was nervous about training me. I was new to Dialysis but not to nursing as you know so I reassured her that she was doing fine.

Then Marie assigned me to one of the techs to teach me how to canulate, place the needles in patients with peripheral sites. This technician had been around for years. Canulating was very similar to starting and IV. I knew that from watching the techs performance but I was still nervous because it was new to me. I watched a few more techs and then Marie went with me to make sure I knew what I was doing.

Roberta began to complain to me about Marie and other staff members, the confusion, disorganization and the preferential treatment of certain staff members. I did not want to be involved in any mess so I mostly listened and tried to encourage her that things would work out. Then she began to complain to me about me. "You're getting better training than I got. Marie didn't show me that. I had one tech show me one time how to do that". I didn't know what was done before I came. I was not responsible for Roberta's treatment or training. Did you say anything to Marie? Did you tell her you were not comfortable with that yet? I asked. She'd say no. When I'm not comfortable with something I speak up. I ask questions. I told her. Well, she did not like the way they were treating her and she did not like the way I handled myself in the environment we shared.

Roberta turned against me. When she saw that she could not influence me negatively or positively in the situation she began to harass me. She began to stir up trouble for me. Since I'm talking about racism, let me go on record as saying Black on Black prejudice is the worst. The worst thing that we as Black people can do is allow others to divide us. Even if we don't agree about how and what to do we should maintain a united front. Don't get me wrong though. I will not go along with mess to appear united. I can't stand strife and confusion.

Every thing began to go down hill from there. What I'd seen in my dream had come true. We had to wear face shields. Sometimes they were uncomfortable because they impaired our vision, Roberta began to give me mixed or false information to confuse me and cause me stress. I will not go into more detail than this.

I resigned from that company but this time I filed a complaint against this employer for discrimination. Out of all the horrible situations I'd experienced this one topped it off. The more I thought about it and analyzed things; I realized that the people who gave me a hard time were the Philippine staff. They were the click this time. They did not treat all the nurses this way because the other nurses submitted to their intimidation. I would not.

I was sick of it! My boss was given a management position practically right out of nursing school. She had no prior management experience or nursing experience. She had the hook up. In my opinion she had poor management skills. The staff turnover rate was horrible but that didn't seem to matter. I filed a complaint with the EEOC.

Chapter 17

I worked for five years as a CNA, ten years as an LVN and ten years as an RN. I worked my way up the ladder so to speak. I had a lot to offer mainly because I still cared. In my entire career I only knew of one patient who made a complaint against me and the complaint proved to be unfounded. I'd love to say I went out with a bang. I'd love to say I finally became a manager, gained the respect of my peers and lived happily ever after but I can't. Now I was in my forties. The years of standing and walking had taken a toll on my legs and back. I could not and did not want to work the floor any more. Though I was traumatized, I applied for several other management positions but did not get any offers. They were concerned that I moved around too much or did not have enough "management" experience.

In the end I decided I did not want to be a nurse anymore. Circumstance propelled me to become an RN. Circumstances propelled me to seek management positions and now circumstances pushed me out of nursing. I accepted the reality that I wanted to get out of nursing many years before this, not because I no longer cared for people but because I was not allowed to "care" for people. I grieved over the loss of my career. But more than that, I grieved that my career ended the way it did. It was a very difficult time for me.

Thank God I won my unemployment claim with out any problems. That helped to sustain my contribution to my family's income during the investigation of my claim. It took around ten months for the EEOC to investigate my claim.

During that ten month period I was compelled to write this story, The Story of a Black Nurse. I did not know how things were going to end for me but I knew this story would be my nursing epitaph.

Chapter 18

Before I tell you how my story ends, let me tell you what happened to the Gardens!

About 2 years later, a friend called me and asked. "Did you hear about what happened to the Gardens"? No, I replied. "Oh it was in the paper and everything"! "They got shut down"! What? I couldn't believe my ears! Lord is this true? Did you answer my prayers after all? I'd prayed, Lord if it will not honor you, don't let it be. After I left the Gardens I did not hear anything good about it. They had problem after problem. It was in the local paper. The article was dated May 16, 2005. The article explained how the Gardens was closed due to quality-of care-infractions; neglected patient needs and did not maintain the facility in a safe manner for the patients. They were sited for excessive deficiencies and taken over by new owners. I had to see it with my own eyes so I went to the facility to see for myself. I was surprised to learn from the receptionist that Albertah was the new DON. I should not have been surprised. I felt cheated but decided to congratulate her any way. She refused to see me.

I felt vindicated in some way. Now there was front-page news that supported my version of what happened to me there. It was undeniable that the owners, some ones at the Gardens did not know what they were doing. If any one had any doubts about my performance they would at least have to acknowledge that something else was seriously lacking at the Gardens.

Thank you Jesus! The Bible says, "The effectual fervent prayers of the righteous availeth much. Prayer does change things!

A few months later I was told that right after I quit working at the Villa it was bought out again. Most of the managers were new including the Administrator. Sherrie did retire. Ellen worked as the DON for a short period of time and quit. Again I felt cheated because Ellen, a part time White nurse got the DON position when she didn't really want it. I called to congratulate her. She told me how she was overwhelmed. Then I realized I was not cheated but spared.

By this time my unemployment was tapped out. My hair was falling out due to stress. Our house was in foreclosure. I'd been emotionally and financially devastated but I kept on praying to the Lord for justice. I did not want all of my pain and suffering to be for nothing.

Finally I got the call I'd been praying for. "Mrs. Jones your former employer has agreed to offer you a settlement." It wasn't what I asked for but it was a decent settlement. I won! I was vindicated! Finally someone had to pay for my pain and suffering and we did not lose our house. The Lord avenged me!

I would not wish my experiences on my worst enemy. The price for my stance costs me a great deal but it did not cost me my life. I know that others paid with their lives to gain equality for Blacks in America and it is still a work in progress.

Before these things happened I believed racism was real. Now I know it is alive and flourishing in Central California. I only pray that my story will somehow motivate others to examine the way they treat others and make some changes in their lives as needed.

Racism is a sin! It is respect of persons. The Bible tells believers not to have respect of persons. Do not say to the well-dressed man, come sit here, up front but then say to the lowly man sit her on my footstool. I am not saying that I am lowly. I am not generalizing that blacks are lowly. I am simply saying treat all men and women as equals. No matter if we are believers in Gods word or not, we will all reap what we sow!

Because I know that racism will continue to exist until the Lord returns I say this. There is strength in numbers. To the young Blacks in the United States; I encourage you to explore the option of becoming a nurse. Wether you become as LVN or an RN ... ...

pretty good depending on what area you choose to specialize in. The medical field needs you. Come to the Central Coast.

I transitioned out of nursing and became a Foster Parent. The transition was rough but God was faithful to sustain me and I know he has great blessings in store for me. I am still in the business of serving others so I did not lose that gifting. God knows if I will ever return to nursing. In the meantime I hope and pray that my story will some how

provoke and motivate some of you to re-light the torch and carry it to the finish line. And when you do, restore the "art of caring" to the profession and reinstitute the spirit of excellence that is greatly needed in this ministry.

My prayer is that one-day I will own a Health Care Facility and or open a School of Nursing.

When I do I will establish and manage my facilities with a spirit of Excellency and Caring.

To God be the glory for all the things he has done for me!

ASSISTANT DIRECTOR OF NURSING

PERFORMANCE EVALUATION

EMPLOYEE _Diane Nixon_

CENTER ████ ████ _Care Center_

PAGE 1 OF 2

CLINICAL						COMMENTS
1.	5	④	3	2	1	1) Obtains timely, pertinent info on pts
2.	5	④	3	2	1	2) Initiates plan of correction/corrective action
3.	5	4	③	2	1	
4.	5	④	③	2	1	4) memos in response to weekly summaries, JJO etc.
5.	5	4	③	2	1	

TOTAL _18_ x _20_ = _3.86_   _3.0_ STANDARD

ADMINISTRATIVE						COMMENTS
1.	5	4	③	2	1	N/A
2.	5	4	③	2	1	N/A
★ 3.	5	4	③	2	1	
★ 4.	5	4	③	2	1	done by RN Adm Coordinator
5.	5	4	③	2	1	no opportunity
6.	5	4	③	2	1	7) makes recommendation e.g.: reduction/center level - work c CS coord
7.	5	④	3	2	1	costs from clinical
8.	5	4	③	2	1	not observed
9.	5	4	③	2	1	9 Good working relationship c other depts.
10.	5	④	3	2	1	10) Participates / exerts leadership abilities
11.	5	④	3	2	1	11) Consistent re inservice - enjoys learning
12.	5	4	③	2	1	12 N/A
13.	5	④	3	2	1	13) Continually trys to improve communication
14.	5	4	③	2	1	
15.	5	4	③	2	1	
16.	5	4	③	2	1	
17.	5	4	③	2	1	17 N/A

TOTAL _55_ x _30_ = _16.5_   _15.3_ STANDARD

SUPERVISION						COMMENTS
1.	5	4	③	2	1	1) N/A
2.	5	4	③	2	1	
3.	5	④	3	2	1	3) Good observation skills & utilizes opportunity to educate
4.	5	4	③	2	1	4) N/A
5.	5	④	3	2	1	5) Documentation of Coaching & education accurate/tmel
6.	5	4	③	2	1	
7.	5	4	③	2	1	
8.	5	4	③	2	1	9) initiates corrective action independently
9.	5	④	3	2	1	10) observes all day each day - assuming resp for
10.	5	④	③	2	1	9.0 error comfort or referring to appropriate staff.

TOTAL _34_ x _30_ = _10.2_   _.30_ STANDARD

Recommend 3% Pay ↗

CONSUMER SERVICE						COMMENTS
1.	5	(4)	3	2	1	1) good role model
2.	5	4	(3)	2	1	
3.	5	4	(3)	2	1	
4.	5	4+	(3)	2	1	4) Customer service good - initiating contact meets standards
5.	5	4	(3)	2	1	
6.	5	4	(3)	2	1	
7.	5	4	(3)	2	1	8) Very astute + aware of pt. rights -
8.	5	(4)	3	2	1	utilizes opportunities to educate

TOTAL 26 X 20 = 5.2   4.8 STANDARD

TOTAL SCORE = 35.5   32.1 STANDARD

COMMENTS ON SPECIFIC WORK PERFORMANCE OR WORK HABITS, I.E., ATTENDANCE:
Has recognized situations where employees became defensive re: what she considered an educational issue / Employee felt they were counseled/coached/ reprimanded.
Has taken more active role in staffing - replacing. Assumes responsibility as PCC more than 50% of the time - + scores in the 90th %tile in that standards of performance

ACTION PLAN TO CORRECT WORK PERFORMANCE OR WORK HABITS OR TO SET NEW GOALS (BY WHOM, BY WHAT DATE):
Beaware of Employees previous response to direction/ education - Anticipate confrontation + place discussion appropriately.
Select areas to assume primary responsibility
Review + revise Standards of Performance

SIGNATURES:

EMPLOYEE: (X) D Mixon RN   DATE: 3/18/9?

SUPERVISOR: ▮▮▮▮   DATE:

DEPT HEAD: T Shew ▮▮▮▮   DATE: 3/18/?

CLASSROOM OBSERVATION FORM FOR TEACHING FACULTY
(Must be reviewed with instructor within two weeks of visit)

Name of Faculty Member _Diane Jones_ Course Observed _Nurs. 479_ Date _10/9/98_

Name of Evaluator _Deborah_ ████████ Number of Students Present _10_

Part One: Describe in a narrative paragraph what classroom activities took place during your visit.

Entered Center and had Ms. Jones paged and she responded promptly. She explained that students are in Module 8 of CNA program practicing bedside and basic hygiene care. The instructor is easily accessible and approachable through her pager and by being able to ask questions when she makes her rounds throughout the facility, which is done frequently.

Ms. Jones is soft spoken and has a gentle approach and positive rapport with students and staff. During evaluation observation, the instructor was followed as she continued her rounds. Several times throughout the hour the students needed assistance in clarifying activities of resident, finding and being introduced to the staff aide, and to observe students performing bedside duties such as having RN exchange O2 Tank, reapplying arm splint, and observing their handwashing and bedmaking techniques. . The instructor consistently guided student with answers to their inquiries, and guiding them to resources in chart and Kardex to provide information. The instructor continually tracks student's progress by keeping anecdotal notes and checking students Skill's check-off list. Before student leaves, the instructor asks if they are comfortable with the instructions and the task at hand.

This particular facility has 110 bed capacity and 3 large Dinning rooms. After breakfast, Instructor took trays from meal carts and had students practice calculating percentage of intake for food and liquids. This was a very good example of having hands on practice and learning application.

Ms. Jones has students stop at 1400 and gives them a half hour to research their next week's resident and at 1430 they have post-conference to review the day's activities and also a possible demonstration of skills, not frequently seen.

My hour went by very quickly and I left very impressed at the fine instruction that Ms. Jones is giving to the ████████ Certified Nursing Aides students.

Part Two: After completing the narrative, please indicate the extent to which the instructor fulfills each of the criteria listed by choosing one of the following categories. Add comments when appropriate.

SA=Strongly Agree   A=Agree   D=Disagree   SD=Strongly Disagree   NA=Not Applicable

		SA	A	D	SD	NA	Comments
1.	The instructor appears enthusiastic and interested in the day's activities.	☐	☑	☐	☐	☐	
2.	The objectives of the day's lesson or activities were clear.	☑	☐	☐	☐	☐	
3.	The instructor displayed expertise in subject matter appropriate to the assigned discipline.	☑	☐	☐	☐	☐	
4.	The instructor conducted class in such a way as to stimulate thinking in students.	☐	☑	☐	☐	☐	
5.	The instructor encouraged students to express their ideas and to become involved.	☑	☐	☐	☐	☐	
6.	The instructor was responsive to students' questions and concerns.	☑	☐	☐	☐	☐	
7.	The instructor presented material which is consistent with existing course outlines.	☑	☐	☐	☐	☐	
8.	The instructor showed an awareness of different teaching/learning styles (variety in presentation).	☐	☑	☐	☐	☐	
9.	The instructor presented material in an organized, easy-to-follow manner.	☐	☑	☐	☐	☐	
10.	Overall, this instructor was effective in the classroom on this day.	☑	☐	☐	☐	☐	

Date of Review: 10/9/98

Signature Instructor _Nanc A. Jones_

Signature Evaluator _Deborah_ ▬▬▬▬ RN, MSN

148

Dixie Jones

INSTRUCTOR TICKET SUBJECT TITLE   NUMBER OF FORMS   18 (0000)

QUESTION NUMBER	QUESTION		SA	A	D	SD	NA	G.P.A. ST-DEV
1	The instructor seems well prepared for class. (Preparation and Organization)	−	4	2	6	6		1.17
2	The instructor seems to enjoy teaching.(Enthusiasm)	+	5	7	5	1		.90
3	I understand the instructors explanations.(Clarity)	½	4	5	3	6		1.20
4	The instructor encourages me to ask questions or make comments in class.(Respect;Encouraging Discussion/Diversity)	½	5	4	5	4		1.15
5	The instructor makes learning this subject interesting. (Interest)	½	3	6	7	2		.92
6	My instructor grades my work fairly.(Fairness of evaluation)	+	7	4	3	4		1.22
7	I feel the workload for this course is reasonable.(Workload)		5	10	2	1		.80
8	I know what is expected of me in this course. (Clarity of objectives)	+	10	5	3			.78
9	My instructor makes helpful comments on my work. (Helpfulness, Feedback)	½	4	5	3	6		1.20
10	I attend class regulary.		15	2	1			.55
11	I participate in class discussions or activities	+	11	7				.58
12	I am taking this course to meet a requirement.		13	2	3			.78
13	I am satisfied with my progress in this course.	+	10	7		1		.78
14	I have learned a lot in this course.(Overall course)	+	9	8		1		3.39 .78
15	Overall, I think this instructor is a good teacher. (Overall instructor)	½	5	4	5	4		2.56 1.15
* FINAL *			110	78	46	36		1.06

Composit	G.P.A.	ST-DEV			G.P.A.	ST-DEV
Overall course	3.51	.62		Overall Instructor	3.62	.52

Life, Physical, and Health Sciences

November 5, 1998

After reviewing Ms. Jones student evaluations we spoke at great length two separate times. The first time, I called reporting that both Ellen ▮▮▮▮ and I had concerns due to the many negative reports. At this time, Ms. Jones had not yet been able to see her score sheet. Thus, we spoke a second time after she had had a chance to get her own report. She also was greatly concerned and did a lot of soul searching as to why she was perceived in a negative light. She wants to readily respond to the students to find out reasons and events that produced these negative feelings. She sincerely, wants to teach, uphold ▮▮▮▮ standards and be a facilitator. She did not respond to the evaluation the next time she saw the students because she felt emotionally upset. But when she does she plans to explain that she needed to make it clear from day one that when she makes a requests and it is not followed, that after three reminders students will be written up (This pertains to duties clinically). She is going to clarify allegations of having an "attitude" by outright asking students for examples and events of such behavior. Her intentions is to not portray an "attitude" and she would appreciate verbal or written response (anonymously) to curb and correct this negative effect. She is also going to consciously make effort to keep her expectations at CNA level instead of moving these students to LVN/RN level beyond their capacity. I reviewed this plan with Ellen ▮▮▮▮ and we are both satisfied with Ms. Jones efforts to strengthen her teaching skills.

Submitted by Deborah ▮▮▮▮

Deborah ▮▮▮▮

DIANE JONES

INSTRUCTOR ████████   TICKET 4295-L SUBJECT NURS 412   TITLE Certified Nursia   NUMBER OF FORMS   12 (0013)

QUESTION NUMBER	QUESTION	SA	A	B	SB	NA	G.P.A. ST-DEV
1	The instructor seems well prepared for class. (Preparation and Organization)	4	8				.49
2	The instructor seems to enjoy teaching. (Enthusism)	5	6	1			.65
3	I understand the instructors explanations. (Clarity)	5	7				.51
4	The instructor encourages me to ask questions or make comments in class. (Respect;Encouraging Discussion/Diversity)	7	4			1	.50
5	The instructor makes learning this subject interesting. (Interest)	6	5	1			.67
6	My instructor grades my work fairly. (Fairness of evaluation)	6	5	1			.67
7	I feel the workload for this course is reasonable. (Workload)	5	6	1			.65
8	I know what is expected of me in this course. (Clarity of objectives)	9	3				.45
9	My instructor makes helpful comments on my work. (Helpfulness, Feedback)	7	5				.51
10	I attend class regularly.	9	3				.45
11	I participate in class discussions or activities	5	7				.51
12	I am taking this course to meet a requirement.	8	3	1			.67
13	I am satisfied with my progress in this course.	9	3				.45
14	I have learned a lot in this course. (Overall course)	9	3				3.75 .43
15	Overall, I think this instructor is a good teacher. (Overall instructor)	5	6	1			3.33 .65
* FINAL *		99	74	6		1	.56

Composit   G.P.A.   ST-DEV
Overall course   3.78   .43   Overall Instructor   G.P.A.   ST-DEV
                                                               3.58   .51

PERSONNEL ACTION NOTICE

☐ New Hire/Start   ☑ Modification   ☐ Annual/Prob. Review   ☐ Termination
   Date: _____   Effective: 9/14/99   Effective: _____   Effective: _____

Name: __Diane Jones_____   EE#: _____

Address: _____
         Street   City/State/Zip

Home Phone: _____   Position: _____

Department: _____   Immediate Supervisor: _____

Total Weekly Hours: _____ FTEs: _____   Schedule: _____

Must be completed for all new employees

SSN: _____   Fed/State Allowance: _____   Date of Birth: _____
                                        (From W4)

Pay Rate Information: $_____ Per Hour/Month
                           $_____ Per Diem Amount (If applicable)
                           $_____ Total Hourly/Monthly Compensation

Pay Increase Information: $ 21.60 Current Pay Rate
                           $ 1.08 Amount of Increase
                           $ 22.68 Total New Base Rate
                           5 % Percentage of Change

                           $_____ Per Diem Amount (If applicable)
                           $_____ Total Pay Rate

Reason for Increase/Adjustment:
__annual review - merit increase_____
_____

Reason for Action/Termination:
_____
_____
_____
_____

_____   _____Paul ████████ 9/24/99
Employee   Date   Supervisor   Date

_____   _____
Administration   Date   Human Resources   Date

JOB DESCRIPTION

DEPARTMENT: Education
DATE: June 14, 1997
JOB TITLE: Nurse Educator
REPORTS TO: Director, Education
JOB SUMMARY: The primary purpose of your job position is to assist in planning, instructing, evaluating, and coordinating the nurse assistant pre-certification program and employee inservice education program implemented by this facility in accordance with current federal and state guidelines.

RESPONSIBILITIES

1. NURSE ASSISTANT PRE-CERTIFICATION: presents a quality nurse assistant pre-certification program, using the approved curriculum.

   a. Participates in and/or assist Director, Education, in constructing class schedules, clinical training schedules, orientation programs for the nurse assistant pre-certification program.

      You have completed this task thoroughly and well.

   b. Provides instruction of the nurse assistant pre-certification program, according to Casa Dorinda's approved curriculum.

      Your success in completing this task is demonstrated in the successful completion and subsequent certification of the last class of nurse assistants. The students and staff were very complimentary in regard to your instruction.

   c. Directly supervises nurse assistant pre-certification students during clinical practice.

      You supervised the students with safety professionalism and efficacy in mind.

   c. Ensures that nurse assistant pre-certification students follow established departmental policies and procedures, including safety regulations and appropriate dress code.

      As above

f. Assists the Director Education in the development and implementation of in-service education programs for employees that meet the facility safety, organizational, regulatory and other identified needs.

Yes, as above.

g. Participates and assists in departmental studies and projects as assigned or that may become necessary.

Yes, including initiating projects that were needed.

3. PROFESSIONAL DEVELOPMENT: maintains expertise in the areas of clinical Management of the geriatric resident and education for the adult learner.

a. Remains current on new developments by attending professional institutions, reading professional journals, and attending professional seminars.

You have attended professional seminars, including "out-of-town" seminars as needed.

b. Maintains professional licensure on active status, and Director of Staff Development State Certification.

Yes

c. Networks with peers within the organization and the community at large.

Yes

4. BUDGET AND PLANNING FUNCTIONS: assists the Director Education in planning the annual budget needs of the training program.

Yes

5. OTHER DUTIES: as assigned, from time to time, by the immediate supervisor.

I am very appreciative of your ability to take initiative to complete functions as needed and to complete tasks with minimal training required.

Management retains the discretionary right to add or change the duties of this position at any time.

6. SUPERVISORY RESPONSIBILITY: nurse assistant pre-certification students

GENERAL STANDARDS

1 - Below Standards   2 - Meets Standards   3 - Exceeds Standards

ATTENDANCE AND RELIABILITY

Can be relied upon to work at assigned times; is conscientious and attentive to job requirements:

	1	2	3
Does not abuse or take advantage of personal time off.	☐	☑	☐
Always provides proper notification for absence or tardiness.	☐	☐	☑
Is willing to adjust personal schedule to complete work load when requested.	☐	☐	☑
Consistently is ready to work at the start of the assigned shift. Requires no "wake up" time.	☐	☐	☑
Takes corrective action to prevent recurring absence.	☐	☐	☑
When "On Call" remains available and responds in a timely manner.	☐	☐	☐ NA
Always gives attention to department policies and follows department procedures.	☐	☐	☑

JUDGEMENT AND DECISION MAKING

Decisions reflect good judgement and are always in the best interest of Casa Dorinda. Is aware of the affect of actions on others:

	1	2	3
Always attempts to understand organizational & resident needs and responds accordingly.	☐	☐	☑
Seeks guidance and direction as necessary for the performance of duties.	☐	☐	☑
Recognizes how the employee's position and duties relate to the overall function of Casa Dorinda.	☐	☐	☑

JUDGEMENT AND DECISION MAKING CONTINUED

	1	2	3
Consistently demonstrates an ability to assess a situation, consider alternatives and choose an appropriate course of action.	☐	☐	☑
Makes no hasty decision and, when appropriate, consults supervisor with any questions.	☐	☐	☑
Accepts new procedures and activities introduced by the Administrator or Department manager.	☐	☐	☑

RELATIONSHIPS WITH OTHERS

Develops and maintains a friendly and professional relationship with those whom employee has contact with:

	1	2	3
Always greets resident, their families, visitors and co-workers in a courteous and friendly manner.	☐	☐	☑
Has established a good rapport and is cooperative with all members of the department.	☐	☐	☑
Always works well with supervisors and those in positions of authority.	☐	☐	☑
Always attempts to understand the needs of others when they request services from the department; demonstrates careful judgement in responding to request.	☐	☐	☑
Always provides direction to residents, their families and visitors in a courteous and positive manner.	☐	☐	☑
Handles telephone information and requests with timeliness courtesy, accuracy and respectfully.	☐	☐	☑

PLANNING AND TIME UTILIZATION

Strives to complete tasks in most efficient manner possible to eliminate "Wasted Time":

	1	2	3

Consistently prioritizes and coordinates activities to

achieve maximum productivity and efficiency during
assigned shift.

☐ ☐ ☑

PLANNING AND TIME UTILIZATION CONTINUED

	1	2	3
Is willing to adjust to revised work schedule as requested in view of workload, emergencies, etc.	☐	☐	☑
Consistently demonstrates the ability to recognize and deal with priorities first and plan for the completion of remaining duties.	☐	☐	☑
Always makes the best use of time during assigned shift.	☐	☐	☑

INITIATIVE

Performance demonstrates that employee is self motivated and acts in the best interest of Casa Dorinda:

	1	2	3
Consistently performs duties in independent manner with minimum supervision.	☐	☐	☑
Assists others in work as required in the department.	☐	☐	☑
Completes all assignments; does not perform just those tasks that are most appealing.	☐	☐	☑
Reports suggestions for positive changes of department policies, procedures or recommendations to department supervisors.	☐	☐	☑
Informs supervisor of situations needing the attention of other department supervisors.	☐	☐	☑
Always uses initiative in following safety procedures to prevent accidents from occurring.	☐	☐	☑
Always reports required repairs and maintenance to department supervisor.	☐	☐	☑
Assumes responsibility for the cleanliness of the work place; does not leave things for someone else to clean up.	☐	☐	☑

Reports safety hazards that are beyond employees control. ☐ ☐ ☑

OTHER BEHAVIORAL FACTORS

Employees knowledge and activity reflect that observance of Casa Dorinda policies are being followed:

	1	2	3
Always observes the department dress code and wears the appropriate personal identification or outer garment.	☐	☐	☑
Has the required understanding of personnel safety and disaster procedures, as contained in the appropriate manuals, reviews the manuals annually and is familiar with personal role.	☐	☐	☑
Attends to personal affairs on own time to avoid disrupting the work schedule.	☐	☐	☑

Demonstrates responsibility for attending required inservice programs and initiative for increasing perso skill level:

Attends inservice training programs as required.	☐	☐	☑
Willingly seeks out and actively participates in the demonstration of new equipment and procedures.	☐	☐	☑
Suggests topics for inservice training to supervisors when a need is identified.	☐	☐	☑

Completes time cards according to department procedures:

Consistently punches time card correctly (including punching in and out for meal times).	☐	☐	☑
Never takes time card out of facility.	☐	☐	☑
Time card is consistently accurate, complete and submitted on time.	☐	☐	☑

Comment on employee's major strengths, contributions made and development achieved since the last performance review.

Your proffessionalism and attention to detail have been an asset to the Education Department and ▓▓▓ ▓▓▓▓
I feel fortunate to have you on our team.
Thank-you for a job well done.

Indentify areas in which employee should seek to improve performance. If overall evaluation is "below standard", list steps the employee must take inorder to continue employment. (Employee must be evaluated again in 3 months).

No substandard areas identified

Additional comments:

Overall evaluation:

☑ Outstanding   ☐ Average/Meets standard   ☐ Needs improvement/Below Standard

Employee comments:

Caul ▓▓▓▓▓▓▓▓
Supervisor/Reviewer Signature

_9/24/99_
Date

Diane A Jones
Employee's Signature

_9/24/99_
Date

5/18/01

To Carol ██████████/Human Resources/Sally/Susan

I have been offered and have accepted a part time position as the Director of Nurses of a new facility that is opening in Lompoc. It is part time because it has not opened yet. The projected opening date is July 1. The last time I checked my PAN was never changed to reflect my 3 day a week schedule so I will return to working 2 days a week beginning 5/23/01. I will work Wednesday and Friday until I have a more definite date to start working full time for ██████████. I will submit my two weeks notice at that time.

I have worked nearly 3 years for ████ and have enjoyed the benefits of a good hourly wage and flexibility in my schedule. For that I am appreciative. I have gained valuable information about managing and how not to manage as well as new insight to my own character.

When I entered this profession at the age of seventeen I discovered right away that the patients were not being cared for properly nor were the CNAs being paid adequately. I told myself that one day I would open my own facility and it would not be ran based on profit or greed.

Five years later, nearly burnt out and disappointed with the medical field I returned to school and became an LVN. After working in acute care I told myself I did not want to work in management because of all the politics, mistreatment of employees and working conditions. Ten years later I became an RN and have gained even more knowledge and learned that the lack of money is not always the reason for poor performance in facilities.

I had long forgotten my dream of owning my own facility. With this new opportunity my hope has been rekindled. My Father reminded me that he never forgot, that if you are dedicated and loyal in the little things you will receive the increase. I now have the chance to start something from the ground up. I can set the standard and truly be responsible for the outcomes. He directed me to a company that has the same philosophies as I do, our goal is to reform nursing, bring back a standard of care based on integrity and treating a person the way you'd want to be treated. In order to do this one must first set the example, teach and train then hold persons accountable for the information they have been given.

I truly believe that all of our experiences in life are for a reason and for a season and I know that I have given my best performance to ██████████ while employed here. I am looking forward to the future.

Sincerely

Diane Jones RN DSD

8/17/01

Board

Montecito, CA

Dear Mr.

I am a 38-year-old wife, mother and minister who happen to also be a black professional. I have been in the medical field for 20 plus years. My career began at the entry level of CNA. Through many obstacles and great adversity I managed to become an RN. I have matured in every area of my life including my profession thus I have earned a certain amount of respect. I have not let the obstacle of my race stop me from pursuing my dreams. In most situations that I have dealt with I have not assumed that my race was the first reason for my problems although that may have always been a factor. I always acknowledged that there was room for growth in me so I chose rather to fight back by being the best that I could be at what I do.

I now find myself in a situation that I have been forced to investigate the possibility that my mistreatment is truly related to prejudice and cultural bias. I worked at a beautiful facility in Montecito Ca. called ████ ████████ where I was the only black woman and black professional woman. To my knowledge we had 200 – 300 hundred employees. There were only two black employees of which I was one. I was there two and a half years. I was hired to be the Assistant Nurse Educator and to work 2 days a week. Although I was only hired to work 2 days a week I mostly worked 3days a week and four when needed for special projects. The majority of that time my workspace was down in the basement parking lot where I shared a classroom with my boss. She had all the necessary items to work comfortably. I housed my personal belongings as well as my work related projects in a storage closet. I could not and did not receive my messages nor were my request to take care of these things ever taken seriously. I taught classes for the facility, which required me to keep records. My boss told me that I would be getting a desk but she had to make sure that I would work out first. That was over two years ago. As you know this facility has good financial resources and all the latest technology. Montecito is a very exclusive community. The person who hired me

163

(Diane ████████) told me that the people here were bigots and just wanted me to be prepared. She later told me that she was very impressed with me because I was the only black person on this campus but yet I walked around with my head held high. She is no longer with the company. She was not liked by several of the staff. I don't know all the details to that situation so I won't elaborate on it any further. I do know that it seemed to be the norm to rally against the people they did not like, make their life unbearable and either cause them to quit or get them fired.

There were many problems in that facility related to lack of supervision and training. During my teaching sessions I faced hostility and resentment because I actually monitored my students training. I was told Carol never did that. Carol was my boss. I reported my problems to my boss. She gave me little to no support. After two years of dealing with this and other issues I felt the professional responsibility to tell the Executive Director of the problems that I was facing as well as some of the other facility problems. I typed a report that took me several days to complete and submitted it to him on April 10th, 2001. He replied that he was disappointed and surprised by my comments and that he would give the matter his careful attention over the next few weeks. That was 4/11/01. I did not here from him again.

On Jan. 16, 01 the Nursing Director (Sally) requested my assistance to train and supervise the staff in an extended capacity. She stated that she liked my style my way of doing things. I also had the background and the experience and that the employees would not be able the manipulate me. We decided that I needed to be visually present in order to be effective so I finally got a work space with a desk area, phone etc. She explained to me that the staff would be resentful (which I already knew) they were not used to being supervised and they would not like my being there. She also explained that we would no longer be catering and explaining ourselves to the employees but that they would have to get in line or we would let them go. The problems that we were dealing with were affecting our ability to provide good care and to retain staff. The CNAs were actually running the place. Instead of going in as a dictator I opted to hold meetings with the staff in which I introduced myself and explained what my new role would be. I thought it would be less threatening. After several meetings I proceeded to make corrections and deal with issues per day-to-day events. I am a soft spoken but direct person who takes pride in my ability to communicate. I am not demanding or forceful in my approach. From the onset of this expanded role I have been challenged, black balled and treated with insubordination by my subordinates those that I am supposed to be teaching and training. The day I moved into my new office. The CNAs on that shift gathered at the Nurses Station and openly complained about me taking their charting area. They were upset and even approached me about it before I had a chance to get settled in. This behavior continued. When Sally was not present they openly blatantly refused to be directed concerning their everyday assignments. Two of them gathered others and complained about me at the station in front of residents and staff and said they would not do what they were being asked to do until they had a chance to talk to Sally. Sally was away on family business. This resulted in several staff members getting written warnings and one getting terminated. Although I sought counsel from the supervisor (Susan) that was acting in the Directors place and from Human Resources (Dorrie) Sally did not support me. She told me I was wrong for doing what I did. And that she did not like other people being involved in the affairs of the Med Center. The Employee handbook says to go to HR if unable to resolve issues via your supervisor. That did not help my situation any. The staff became more hostile and more resentful. Several staff members have told me that I am dealing with a cultural issue, "they feel that if you explain things to them that you are talking down to them." They have told me personally that they don't like the way I tell them what do. I reported this too the Director. She did not agree with this possibility. At a staff meeting some CNAs accused me of being inflexible. They were upset because I made rounds and checked to see if the cleaning assignments had been done. A few of them had not been done so I proceeded to assist some of the staff in completing the assignments. They felt that I should not have checked because they had to attend an in-service that day. My perspective was different I felt that because the in-service had been held at four different times that day, we had 18-20 RN nursing students in the building also providing bed side care (not to mention the fact that quite a few of the CNAs had the assistance of Private Duty aides to help them with their resident's care, something that is against DHS regulations). We had more than enough help. The place should have been in tiptop shape. I do not accept these types of excuses when the evidence is factually to the contrary. Sally informed me that there have been complaints against me. She said, "It is nothing that they can quite put their finger on." Neither she nor they could give me any examples of rude behavior on my part.

The CNA's are predominately of Latino and Hispanic decent so I have sought council from other Hispanics whom I considered to be professional if not in there title at least in their behaviors. I wanted to know if we should host some cultural awareness classes to promote better working relations. The people I talked to did not think it was necessary to hold classes but rather felt the staff was just not used to being supervised and did not like it. I have talked to all the appropriate Department heads concerning my issues (Social Services, Director of Education, Human Resources, The Executive Director, and the Director who asked me to do this job). The Director said she could not give me any advice or suggestions on how to proceed from this point except that I let the other supervisor be the bad guy for a while. The other supervisor has only been a RN for two and a half years and she had never worked in a skilled care facility (SNF). She is just now learning the State and Federal regulations required for this type of facility. She is also direct but is more abrupt in her approach. I know she has made people cry but the Director told me she has a more positive approach then I do. She assured me that she still felt I was the person for the job and that I was doing a good job. The staff was working better, they were attending training classes more and the residents where reporting that they were getting better care. I called the HR Director and informed her of this conversation. I asked if I had done something wrong and she assured me I had not. I told her that I was asked to do this job but now I am not being supported. I did not know if I should give up the position or not. She informed me that she would talk to her boss about it. A week or so later I asked her if she heard any thing. She informed me that her boss (Emma) was going to talk to the Executive Director about it. I never got a response. I took the advice of the Director and began to refer all problems and issues to the other supervisor or to her. After several days I followed up with the Director and expressed my feelings regarding her suggestions. I informed her that she asked me to do this job and that I needed to be supported by her. She said she would be more supportive but the next time I reported an incident to her in which I felt that I was being verbally attacked by a CNA for simply doing my job she never addressed the situation or gave me any feedback (5/11/01). I went home in tears that day. (Not the first time)

I was followed around by Sally's sister (Judy) she was an activity Director. The CNAs confided in her she kept them stirred up against me and reported my every move back to her sister Sally. I asked her not to be involved with nursing issues because this was not her department and to refer the nursing staff to Susan or my self. We were trying to establish a chain of command.

I believe in giving praise as well as constructive feedback when I'm supervising but whenever I praised any of my former students for good work I was accused a having favorites. Judy even approached me very upset and accused me of causing the activities program to suffer because I required the staff to attend in-services something that up until then they thought was optional. In-services are required by the Department of Health. When other functions were going on such as parties or employee pot lucks the staff was used to leaving the residents unattended. I attempted to require some structure in these areas. Judy did not like that because she was used to being able to tell the CNAs what to do.

Several of the Nurses told me that they were afraid to say anything to the CNAs because they would be black balled. One had even been cornered in a room and threatened. I have faced other issues in jobs before but never have I been so disrespected and mistreated for doing a good job. CNAs are only permitted to work in skilled care facilities under a licensed nurse. The nurses had the responsibility of the CNAs but very little support when it came to monitoring their performance. They reported to me that Sally would Hide in her office at crucial times and that she would not do anything about the warnings and write ups they gave her concerning poor job performance. The CNAs took long lunches on the clock and took lunches at the same time leaving the floor unattended. This was a regular occurrence on the PM shift. A PM shift nurse informed me that for the first time in several years she was glad to see the CNAs actually working when they arrived at work instead of wasting the first two hours socializing. She got down on her knees, kissed my hand and thanked me for all my help. She was one of the people who were afraid to say anything to them before I came to help supervise.

I kept Sally informed continually of my activities. She supported me in private and then I took all the heat.

5/16/01 I was offered and accepted a new position to be the DON at another facility. I informed my boss and the other supervisors that I would continue to work part time for ███████until I had further information regarding when my new position would become full time. Even though it has been a very uncomfortable environment to work in I wanted to handle things appropriately. They did not give me any feedback but rather acted as though they did not know or care about this new information. I called my boss to ask her if she got my letter she said she had not but said the Director approached her concerning the matter.

On 5/24/ 01 a nurse who had just gotten fired warned me that she heard I was also fired last week. I informed her that I was not fired but took a few days off because of the stress I was experiencing at work. She told me to walk softly then because they are looking for a way to fire you. When I returned to work (5/30) I went to HR and inquired as to weather or not this rumor was true. She denied it but stated that she would check with the Director about it. Later on that day I was let go. My position was suddenly deleted. I was given severance pay and told that this was best for all concerned since I was leaving anyway. I expressed my disappointment at being treated so badly while I was employed here (not the first time) they assured me that they felt anyone who had accepted this position would have been treated that way. I replied that there was some truth to that but other staff informed me that this was cultural too. The Director informed me that she did not agree with this but felt my problems there were more political than anything and I needed to learn to play the political game and choose my battles more wisely. I should add that I was told one of the other staff nurses is now assisting with the position that I held. (Supposedly the position was deleted also because they did not need another supervisor).

Considering the way I was treated I am inclined to pursue my inquiry into this matter with you. I do not wish to pursue this now only for myself but for any other person, or persons who have had to endure such mistreatment. I believe that we have either been discriminated against because we did not fit into the cultural bias and or because we did not conform to the low work standard that the others were perpetuating. The few Hispanics (4 all together) that I know were mistreated were mistreated because they were in my class. I trained them and they accepted a professional standard of care from me and refused to compromise. Eventually two of them did give in to the pressure. I feel that no matter what the individual's personal feelings are one should not be discriminated against for either reason.

I believe I was set up to fail. I was used as a scapegoat. I lost several nights of sleep. I cried many tears and was humiliated by my co- workers. The day that I was let go I was in a daze. My husband followed me home to assure my safety. When I made it home I began to feel chest pains due to hyperventilating.

Please give me your opinion and attention concerning this matter?

I have enclosed a copy of my Resume intended to show my professional background

Respectfully

Diane S. Jones

September 13, 2001

Diane S. Jones
3617 Via Orilla
Lompoc, CA 93436

Dear Mrs. Jones:

Your letter of August 17, 2001, to Dr. ████████████ was referred to me, as Chairman of the Board of Directors of the Montecito ████████████████, for reply.

We at ████████████ are extremely proud of our record of positive employee relationships and we endeavor at all times to maintain a positive atmosphere and supportive environment within our campus community. Consequently, we take the comments in your letter very seriously and I have directed the Executive Director to undertake an investigation of the pertinent facts and circumstances.

We were pleased to note from your current resume that you have been successful in securing a Director of Nursing position in Lompoc, where you live, that affords to you not only a full-time position, but also one with significantly more responsibilities than you held with us.

Thank you for taking the time to write to us. Please accept our very best wishes for your future endeavors.

Very truly yours,

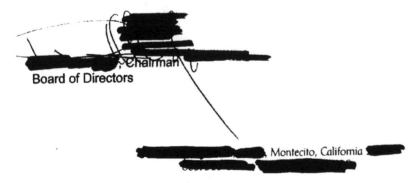

, Chairman
Board of Directors

Montecito, California

Gardens

Lompoc, California

EMPLOYEE PERFORMANCE APPRAISAL

Name: DIANE JONES   Review Date: 12/26/01

Position: DON   Date of Last Review: NA

Department: NURSING   Type of Review: 90 day

Process:
The appraisal is completed by the immediate Supervisor. The evaluator is to complete each section and discuss the appraisal with the employee. The employee should sign the appraisal, indicating he/she has read the appraisal. The evaluation should also be reviewed by the Department Head. The employee receives a copy and the original is placed in the personnel file.

Criteria:

5	Outstanding	3	Satisfactory	1	Unsatisfactory
4	Very Good	2	Needs Improvement		

SECTION 1 INDIVIDUAL PERFORMANCE

Quality of Work:
Produces complete and accurate work.   5 ④ 3 2 1

Comments:

_____

_____

Quantity of Work:
Produces high volume of work.   5 ④ 3 2 1

Comments:

_____

_____

Dependability:

Depended upon to be available for work.	5 ④ 3 2 1
Excellent attendance record.	⑤ 4 3 2 1
Starts work promptly.	5 4 ③ 2 1
Remains at work location as required.	⑤ 4 3 2 1
Maintains confidentially.	⑤ 4 3 2 1
Follows directions.	⑤ 4 3 2 1

171

Comments:

Sometimes late for meetings, setting own personal schedule

Interpersonal Skills:

The ability to effectively interact with others to accomplishment a task.	5 ④ 3 2 1
Adapts to changing situations well.	5 ④ 3 2 1
Willing to assist others in accomplishing additional work.	5 ④ 3 2 1
Is receptive to constructive criticism.	5 ④ 3 2 1
Considers viewpoints of others.	⑤ 4 3 2 1
Cooperates with other employees in a pleasant and courteous manner.	⑤ 4 3 2 1
Handles difficult situations in a tactful manner.	⑤ 4 3 2 1

Comments:

Diplomacy in dealing with others is excellent.

Organization Skills:

The ability to establish a clear, concise, step-by-step pattern of accomplishing one's work.	5 ④ 3 2 1
Maintains an organized work area and coordinates work flow appropriately.	5 ④ 3 2 1
Manages time effectively and meets deadlines.	⑤ 4 3 2 1
Pays attention to detail.	⑤ 4 3 2 1
Works well under pressure.	5 ④ 3 2 1
Anticipates and coordinates activities.	⑤ 4 3 2 1
Recognizes priorities.	⑤ 4 3 2 1

Comments:

Problem Solving:

The ability to analyze problems effectively and determine Appropriate action for their solution.	5 ④ 3 2 1
Identifies existing problems.	5 ④ 3 2 1
Anticipates and identifies potential problems.	5 ④ 3 2 1
Considers possible alternatives.	⑤ 4 3 2 1
Knows how and where to obtain necessary information.	5 ④ 3 2 1
Makes thoughtful recommendations.	⑤ 4 3 2 1

Comments:

_____

_____

_____

Initiative:

The ability to contribute, develop and
   carry out new ideas or methods.   5 4 ③ 2 1

Works with minimum supervision.   ⑤ 4 3 2 1

Offers suggestions for improvements.   5 ④ 3 2 1

Seeks additional responsibilities.   5 ④ 3 2 1

Carries out work projects without prompting, once briefed.   ⑤ 4 3 2 1

Comments:

_____

_____

_____

Communication Skills:

Listens effectively and provides clear, concise, and accurate
   verbal and written information to groups or individuals in
   appropriate and timely manner.   ⑤ 4 3 2 1

Comments:

_____

_____

_____

SECTION 2 OVERALL PERFORMANCE EVALUATIONS:

Strengths:

Describe major assets, skills or achievements.

Highly motivated self-starter who requires little supervision.
Seeks additional responsibility. Good cooperative attitude.
Pleasure to work with. Teachable.

Areas requiring further development:

Describe the areas in the employee's performance that need further development.

Computer skills need to be improved for efficient management
of staffing, good record-keeping.
Performance to this point has been outside of expected
job skills & requirements, therefore 90-day probation will
be extended to allow for observation under more normal
conditions. Recommend further 90 day probation period,
starting 27 December 01.

Indicate plans to develop or improve the employee's performance, with a timetable for implementation.

Subject and Type of Plan   Tentative Timetable

EMPLOYEE COMMENTS:

Signatures:

Diane A Jones
Employee   12/26/01
                                                Date

Supervisor   26 Dec 01
                                                Date

Diane served as Interim Administrator and ~~WH~~ Director of Staff Development for a period of three months during startup. She put forth excellent effort and managed three positions well, under adverse circumstances and high pressure, working extra hours when needed.

It was agreed that Diane would become salaried ~~WH~~ as of the present pay period at a rate of $4,333.26 per month. Monthly salary is to increase to $4,500.00 effective March 1, 2002. The next increase will be discussed when the facility reaches profitability.

Gardens

Employee Name: *Diane James*	Social Security Number	Date of Notice: 01-25-02
Facility Name: *Gardens*	Job Title *DON* DOH: 10-1-01	Date of Termination (If applicable) 01-25-02

The intent of this notice is to make you aware of deficiencies in your conduct/performance and give you an opportunity to correct and improve your value to the company. Repeated violation of rules or continued performance/conduct problems, whether related to this situation or not, will result in further disciplinary action, up to and including discharge. *(Not applicable for termination notice)*

| ☐ VERBAL COUNSELING | ☐ WRITTEN WARNING ☐ 1st ☐ 2nd | ☐ SUSPENSION, pending investigation, subject to discharge | ☒ DISCHARGE Last day worked 1/25/02 *(if different from term date)* |

NOTED DEFICIENCY

☐ Attendance
☒ Performance
☐ Resident Care
☐ Safety Rules Violation
  ♦ Was retraining necessary (Y/N) _____
  ♦ Date of retraining
☐ Misconduct (state policy violated)
_____
_____

☒ Discharge as a result of progressive discipline: previous written warnings within past 12 months.
1 *Extended Probation*
2

COMPLETE EXPLANATION of incident(s) resulting in disciplinary action. Attach supporting documents.

Failed to demonstrate adequate experience for the DNS position even after extending initial probationary period.

Employee discharged during extended probation. Discharge witnessed by Steve ▓▓▓

GOALS: corrective action plan, expected goals, & how improvements measured. (Not applicable if Termination)

THIS SITUATION WILL BE REVIEWED AGAIN ON _____ (Date) BY _____

EMPLOYEE COMMENTS:

I have read and received a copy of this Notice. I have been given an opportunity to comment and I am aware of my rights to appeal this action through the Company's Problem Solving Procedures.

Employee's Signature	Date	Signature of Witness/Date (If employee refuse to sign)

APPROVAL

Immediate Supervisor's Signature	Date	Administrator's Signature * *Gracie* ▓▓▓	1/25/02 Date

All terminations for cause must be approved by the Administrator.

L17-G2 (5/98)

PERFORMANCE PLANNING AND APPRAISAL

EMPLOYEE INFORMATION:

DIANE JONES
Name of Employee

10-21-2004
Date

STAFF RN
Job Title

ATLANTA U?LL
Department/Division

Purpose of Review: 3 months / 6 months   Annual   Other _____

PROCEDURE:

SECTION 1 describes eight professional criteria with job success or failure. Check the rating that most closely indicates the level at which the individual has performed. Write the corresponding numerical value in the last column. Add the numbers to obtain a total value.

Transfer the total to the appropriate space at the bottom of the page. This will indicate and support your overall evaluation of the individual's performance.

SECTION 2 provides space for discussing overall job performance. Refer to Section 1 when completing this section.

SECTION 3 should reflect a mutually agreed-upon work plan for the coming review period. This section enables the supervisor and employee to develop a work plan for accomplishing the future objectives.

SECTION 4 is reserved for the individual's comments and signatures.

PROFESSIONAL CRITERIA	Below Job Requirements Performance was below job requirements in one or more important areas and immediate improvement will be required.	Achieved Job Requirements Performance met job requirements in all important areas with extra effort evident in one or more of the following: quality, quantity, timeliness or other important dimensions of performance.	Exceeded Job Requirements		Insert Numerical Value
			Performance exceeded the requirements of the job in several important areas.	Performance exceeded the requirements of the job in all major areas and significant work above and beyond the responsibilities of the job was achieved.	
	0	**1**	**2**	**3**	**(0-3)**
KNOWLEDGE Consider knowledge of skills, procedures, methods, equipment and materials required to do the job.	Inadequate job knowledge. Understanding of the skills, procedures and methods required for job is insufficient	Understands and effectively completes normal job routine. Needs little additional instruction.	Well informed. Completely understands all aspects of this job and related jobs.	An authority on own responsibilities. Knows why job functions are performed and interrelationships with other jobs.	(
PRODUCTIVITY Consider the amount of work the individual actually produces during an extended period of time.	Works at extremely slow pace. Rarely meets deadlines. Needs constant follow up.	Works at a steady pace. Output definitely meets requirements. Occasionally work completed ahead of deadlines.	Works fast. Produces more than most. Often work completed ahead of deadlines.	Exceptional producer. Consistently completes work ahead of deadlines	(
QUALITY Consider the accuracy and thoroughness of employee's work. Assess work results in terms of rejections, errors and overall neatness.	Excessive errors and mistakes. Requires constant checking and rework	Meets standards for accuracy and neatness. Makes some mistakes, but of a tolerable level. Needs normal supervision.	Consistently high degree of accuracy and neatness. Work can be relied upon. Seldom needs supervision.	Consistently highest level of quality. Final output is virtually perfect.	\
INITIATIVE Consider the degree to which employee is a self-starter, can work with minimum supervision, seeks new and better methods to do the job.	Shows little initiative. Never volunteers. Must be told to do everything	Voluntarily solves non-routine job problems when necessary. Effective worker.	Seeks new tasks and responsibilities. Resourceful in familiar situations. Self-starter.	Goes out of way to accept responsibility. Highly resourceful and constructive in new situations.	\

PROFESSIONAL CRITERIA (con't)	Below Job Requirements Performance was below job requirements in one or more important areas and immediate improvement will be required.	Achieved Job Requirements Performance met job requirements in all important areas with extra effort evident in one or more of the following: quality, quantity, timeliness or other important dimensions of performance.	Exceeded Job Requirements		Insert Numerical Value
			Performance exceeded the requirements of the job in several important areas.	Performance exceeded the requirements of the job in all major areas and significant work above and beyond the responsibilities of the job was achieved.	
	0	**1**	**2**	**3**	**(0-3)**
COOPERATION Consider the effectiveness of the employee in accomplishing duties by working with others (e.g. peers, supervisors, customers)	Frequently is hostile and uncooperative when working with others to complete an assigned task. Attitude is unacceptable.	Generally cooperative. Willing to accept suggestions and direction. Acceptable relations with others.	Very cooperative. Usually shows consideration of others' viewpoints. Often offers assistance. Can be counted on to help.	Always works effectively with others. Shows a keen insight into people. Constantly offers and always is available to help others.	1
DEPENDABILITY Consider the extent to which employee can be relied upon to be available for work and to do it properly.	Frequently undependable. Often fails to deliver a complete job. Leaves routine tasks incomplete.	Dependable. Can be relied on to complete all aspects of job. Needs normal supervision.	Very dependable and persistent despite possible difficulties. Completes normal work and occasional special projects with little supervision.	Highly motivated and trustworthy. Can be counted on to go beyond limits of duties with little or no supervision when needed.	1
ORDERLINESS Consider the employee's ability to organize work and work area.	Frequently disorganized with work area in disarray. Results in a high degree of lost time and inefficiency.	Work sufficiently organized to efficiently perform job.	Highly organized and efficient worker.	Exceptionally precise in organization of work. Has immediate access to anything needed. Extremely efficient.	1
ATTENDANCE Consider the employee's record of being at work regularly and on time.	Unacceptable attendance record. Continual lateness or absences from work.	Occasionally is absent or tardy. Reports absence or tardiness in advance.	Seldom absent or tardy. Always reports reports absence or tardiness in advance.	Excellent attendance record. Always at work and on time.	2

OVERALL RATING DETERMINATIONS: Check appropriate box on basis of total points.

☐ Exceeded job requirements in all major areas 22-24 Points   ☐ Exceeded job requirements in several important areas 14-21 Points   ☒ Achieved job requirements 7-13 Points   ☐ Below job requirements 0-6 Points

TOTAL POINTS	9

PERFORMANCE PLANNING AND APPRAISAL

SECTION 2: STRENGTHS & DEVELOPMENT NEEDS:

Cite outstanding accomplishments and describe employee's specific strong points.

- Diane is able to analyze PT; give meds IV, PUT on /take off PT.
- Diane is able to change compenter dressing - using aseptic technique.
- Diane is able to write monthly summaries & in schedule.

Describe areas where the employee must improve or training is needed.

1. specimen labs → packing; labs → other - what is it for.
2. critique
3. blood mixing

SECTION 3: WORK PLAN FOR COMING REVIEW PERIOD: *(if appropriate)*

A.   List objectives or special projects *(in priority)* that have been assigned to the employee for the coming review period. State results or stands of performance and target dates mutually agreed upon. (Attach additional page if necessary).

Diane will be able to do labs → packing

B.   Describe the action plan which will be used to achieve the objectives listed above. (i.e. what staff member, supervisor or others will do and within what time frame)

1. I will have Diane orient by specimen lab processor on how to pack labs.

2. I will be available @ all times for any questions.

SECTION 4: EMPLOYEE COMMENTS & SIGNATURES

EMPLOYEE COMMENTS

Employee's Signature
(Signature does not imply agreement with contents.)

Date 11/26/04

Supervisor's Signature

Date 11/26/04

Other Management Approval

Date 12/2/04